JOHN CHEEVER

A Study of the Short Fiction

Also Available in Twayne's Studies in Short Fiction Series

Twayne's Studies in Short Fiction

Gordon Weaver, General Editor
Oklahoma State University

JOHN CHEEVER

A Study of the Short Fiction

James E. O'Hara
Pennsylvania State University–York

TWAYNE PUBLISHERS • BOSTON
A Division of G. K. Hall & Co.

Twayne's Studies in Short Fiction Series No. 9
Copyright © 1989 by G. K. Hall & Co.
All rights reserved.
Published by Twayne Publishers
A Division of G. K. Hall & Co.
70 Lincoln Street, Boston, Massachusetts 02111

Copyediting supervised by Barbara Sutton.
Book design by Janet Reynolds.
Typeset in 10/12 Caslon by Compset, Inc.

Printed on permanent/durable acid-free paper
and bound in the United States of America.

Library of Congress Cataloging-in-Publication Data

O'Hara, James Eugene.
    John Cheever : a study of the short fiction / James E. O'Hara.
        p.   cm.—(Twayne's studies in short fiction ; no. 9)
    Bibliography: p.
    Includes index.
    ISBN 0-8057-8310-5 (alk. paper)
        1. Cheever, John—Criticism and interpretation.   2. Short story.
    I. Title.   II. Series.
    PS3505.H6428Z8   1989
    813'.52—dc20   89-32877
                                                                               CIP

Contents

Preface

The apparent ease with which gifted artists and master craftsmen exercise their skill can be deceiving. We enjoy their finished work, or watch them move gracefully across the stage or playing field and imagine that almost anyone, with a little practice, could do as well. Sometimes they beguile us with their facility into thinking that a brilliant performance or new painting or piece of sculpture has sprung forth almost spontaneously, "naturally." The best of John Cheever's short stories are creations of this kind.

The gracefulness of these stories, and of many others that are less than brilliant, is in part the trick of a master who knows how to hide the evidence of his effort so that the casual observer will concentrate on the product of his labors. Over a long and difficult lifetime, Cheever learned by experience that only a lucid style would gain him the kind of audience he needed to survive as a writer, just as he learned by daily observation how human beings adapt to the rigors of life, and often overcome them. Such observation furnished him with enough raw material for five novels and a hundred and fifty-four short stories, published between 1930 and 1981.

A discerning reader will find that Cheever raises some of the same disturbing questions about human behavior as those posed by more difficult writers, and often suggests answers that bespeak a serious, probing mind deeply aware of human weakness and ultimately convinced of human strength. Although critics are by no means agreed on the general merits of Cheever's views on the human condition, not even the most vociferous of them would dispute his technical craftsmanship.

After nearly four decades of practicing his storytelling art, and living through several cycles of personal failure and success, Cheever finally came to agree with that most "difficult" of writers, William Faulkner, that "man will not merely endure: he will prevail. He is immortal, not because he alone among creatures has an inexhaustible voice, but because he has a soul, a spirit capable of compassion and sacrifice and endurance."[1] Faulkner, primarily a novelist, discovered a vein of human strength hidden under layers of ignorance and evil in a South haunted by the unburied ghosts of the Civil War. Cheever, primarily a short story writer, worked the equally rich lodes of a New England forever trapped between its allegiance to tradition and its need to break free from the past. Both writers were fully aware of the irony inherent in the notion that the changes wrought by the twentieth century were "improvements." Both could see far enough into the heart of things not to be so easily misled; that was their gift and their curse. Beyond that, similarities cease. Besides his choice of subjects and his frequent use of fantastic effects, Cheever's reliance on poetic devices (rhythm, lyrical repetition, startling images) clearly distinguishes his style from that of Faulkner, or—after 1947—any other writer.

Cheever is usually regarded as a *"New Yorker* writer," specializing in tales of suburban manners and morals or the absence thereof. Stories like "O Youth and Beauty!," "The Sorrows of Gin," "The Swimmer," and "The Brigadier and the Golf Widow" can be cited to bear out the generalization. Just as Faulkner created Yoknapatawpha County and peopled it with beings both comically absurd and deeply tragic, Cheever laid out the geographical and spiritual coordinates of Bullet Park and Shady Hill, and gave us the perplexing characters of Neddy and Lucinda Merrill, Cash Bentley and Johnny Hake. For the most part, these fictional people seem to inhabit a less threatening country than those drawn by Faulkner or Hemingway. They travel by train to the city to work or to be entertained, and they come home to comfortable houses and swimming pools in the suburbs. But what interests us about them, as it certainly interested Cheever, is the inevitable tendency of their lives to spin madly out of control when "something happens."

As in real life, that something can be a genuinely shattering event— a death or illness, the loss of a job—or it can be a chance remark or innocent gesture, rightly or wrongly interpreted. If Cheever's fiction does not often attain the level of seriousness probed by Faulkner, D. H. Lawrence, or Nikolai Gogol, his best work can legitimately be compared with that of such masters as F. Scott Fitzgerald, Katherine Mansfield, and Anton Chekhov. It is probably true that the short story is better suited to the presentation of those minor triumphs and failures that determine the flavor of most of our lives than it is to the exploration of the major events or evolutions that we typically read about in novels. As Cheever himself put it in a 1935 letter to his friend and mentor Elizabeth Ames, "Our lives have not been sustained or constant or ordered. Our characters don't die in bed. The powerful sense of passed and passing time that seems to be the one definable and commendable quality of the novel is not our property. Our lives are not long and well-told stories."[2]

But of all the short story writers that Cheever might be profitably compared to, he is perhaps closest in spirit to one of the nineteenth-century American inventors of the form, Nathaniel Hawthorne. Hawthorne was a theorist as well as a deviser of haunting prose tales, and in the preface to *The Marble Faun* he described the problem faced by American writers of his generation: "No author, without a trial, can conceive of the difficulty of writing a Romance about a country where there is no shadow, no antiquity, no mystery, no picturesque and gloomy wrong, nor anything but a commonplace prosperity, in broad and simple daylight, as is happily the case with my dear native land."[3]

Cheever, writing in the northeastern United States in the twentieth century—well after America's Civil War and Gilded Age, during and after an equally historic period characterized by the Great Depression and two world wars—may have been more fortunate than Hawthorne. His culture had acquired a certain fullness of "picturesque and gloomy wrong" to draw on for narrative material, and creative artists of his generation could travel abroad with greater ease to see and become acquainted with older societies. In Cheever's case, military service in World War II required him to travel in the Pacific, and later his growing reputation opened the door for him to take several visits to Europe. His experiences in both instances bore fruit in some of his most interesting short stories.

But if Hawthorne's complaint was that a shortage of "inherited" material forced him to imagine his own narrative worlds, it is worth noting that a century later, Cheever would deliberately choose to transcend a realistic style that he had perfected (and that, broadly speaking, was part of a general literary trend away from the "artificial" style perfected by Hawthorne and Edgar Allan Poe in the nineteenth century), turning instead to a more imaginative—and occasionally fantastic—narrative technique.

As stylists, of course, Hawthorne and Cheever are leagues as well as years apart. In fact they resemble each other in only one important respect: both are obsessed with the problem of evil as an inescapable part of the human condition. Hawthorne set forth the issue in such stories as "Young Goodman Brown" and "The Maypole of Merry Mount," and at greater length in *The Scarlet Letter.* His explorations of the Calvinist-Puritan view of human corruption are still considered among the most insightful treatments of the early American psyche available to us, although they seem almost quaint when studied from the more liberal perspective of the late twentieth century. Still, the reader of Cheever's stories will often hear in them clear echoes of New England's Puritan past; and his friend John Updike, in reviewing Cheever's last published story (the short novel *Oh What a Paradise It Seems*), correctly observed that "Cheever's instinctive belief in the purity and glory of Creation brings with it an inevitable sensitivity to corruption; like Hawthorne, he is a poet of the poisoned."[4] In the same vein, critic John Leonard has asserted that "Cheever speaks not so much of failures of luck and charm as of failures of faith. How to be brave and good? He mobilizes language in the service of decencies and intuitions that are no longer sanctioned at any altar or practiced in any politics. His stories are brilliant prayers on behalf of 'the perfumes of life: seawater, the smoke of burning hemlock, and the breasts of women.'"[5] Leonard's assessment accurately identifies the universal quality that informs the varied particulars of Cheever's writing—a quality that earned him the admiration of fellow writers as diverse as Updike, Saul Bellow, and John Gardner.

In the following pages, I trace the evolution of John Cheever as a writer of short fiction, examining a representative selection of his stories to clarify significant developments in both the style and thematic content of his work from 1930 to 1981. I demonstrate that after an impressive beginning as a young writer not yet out of his teens, Cheever had to struggle to establish his credentials as an able practitioner of his craft; that following World War II he began to write stories that are stylistically original and more clearly identifiable as the work of an accomplished master; that with increasing popular acceptance and a degree of success there came a period of personal decline, reflected in stories that continue to be technically impressive even as they become steadily more caustic in outlook; and, finally, that after a crisis in his sixty-third year, Cheever was able to recover the sense of spiritual balance that characterizes the best work of his earlier years.

Except for stories specified in the Notes, in-text page references are to *The Stories of John Cheever* (New York: Alfred A. Knopf, 1978).

James E. O'Hara

The Pennsylvania State University–York

Notes

1. William Faulkner, "Speech of Acceptance upon the Award of the Nobel Prize for Literature," *The Faulkner Reader* (New York: Modern Library, 1959), 3–4.
2. "Cheever's Letters," *Vanity Fair,* May 1984, 63.
3. In *The Complete Novels and Selected Tales of Nathaniel Hawthorne,* ed. Norman Holmes Pearson (New York: Random House Modern Library edition, 1937), 589–91. For a further discussion, see also Brian Atterby's *The Fantasy Tradition in American Literature* (Bloomington: Indiana University Press, 1980), 42.
4. "On Such a Beautiful Green Little Planet," *New Yorker,* 5 April 1982, 190.
5. "Cheever Country," *New York Times Book Review,* 7 March 1982, 26.

Acknowledgments

I wish to thank the editors of *Massachusetts Studies in English* for permission to revise my essay "'Independence Day at St. Botolph's': The Wapshot Saga Begins" for inclusion in this volume; I also thank the editors of *Modern Language Studies* for permission to include my essay "John Cheever's Flowering Forth: The Breakthroughs of 1947" (Fall 1987, 50–59) here.

I acknowledge the kindness of Professor Dennis Coates for facilitating my preparation of the Selected Bibliography, and of Professor Scott Donaldson who promptly and generously answered my requests for bibliographical and biographical information.

I have quoted extensively from *The Stories of John Cheever* (New York: Alfred A. Knopf, 1978), © 1978 by John Cheever, and am grateful for the publisher's permission to do so.

The York Campus Advisory Board provided generous financial support for my initial research, and the assistance of Pennsylvania State University's College of Liberal Arts and Faculty Scholarship Support Fund greatly facilitated my efforts.

My gratitude to my editors and to all those who helped in the completion of this book, especially my wife and family, is boundless.

Part 1

THE SHORT FICTION:
A CRITICAL ANALYSIS

Soundings

In a way it was all there for John Cheever from the beginning. He was a natural storyteller even as a child, when he entertained his fellow students by weaving fantasies out of the stuff of his imagination and his limited experience of life. Later he was enrolled at Thayer Academy, a private school, and found the range of his experience growing, but not in the right directions; the young storyteller learned that a student's life can be surprisingly complicated. His unhappiness at Thayer increased until he and the school administration decided to part company. But young Cheever took his storytelling ability with him and decided to use it as a weapon against the kind of miseducation he felt he had experienced.

Cheever wrote "Expelled" when he was still seventeen. It was published in 1930, when he was eighteen, launching a literary career that would span more than half a century. This first story demonstrates the remarkable gifts that, years later, would reappear in his best work: skillful pacing, sharp characterization and place description, and careful thematic development based on a clear narrative viewpoint. For one brief moment, Cheever appeared to be a potential heir to the laurels of Sherwood Anderson and F. Scott Fitzgerald.

But in a way it wasn't quite all there for him, even in 1930. A straightforward reworking of bitter experience, "Expelled" could also be seen as an exercise in self-indulgence. Its submission to Malcolm Cowley at the then-radical *New Republic* was a precocious feat of marketing genius—something Cheever would be unable to repeat for five difficult years. Together he and Cowley had made a bold statement about the stultifying atmosphere of America's educational establishment. The application of the storyteller's talent made the statement into art of a sort, but not necessarily first-rate art. The distinction would have been of little concern to the *New Republic*; the story cut close enough to the bone of reality to interest its left-leaning readers. For Cheever himself, however, the point had great importance, although it is unclear whether he realized it then. If he became a faithful recorder of the events and relationships in his life, rather than a truly creative writer, he would have imposed significant limits on his considerable powers of invention.

"Expelled" is written in the first person, a point of view he virtually abandoned for the rest of his literary apprenticeship. The headnote to the story explains that the author "was expelled from an academy in Massachusetts at the end of his junior year," and that the story will recreate "the atmosphere of an institution where education is served out in dry cakes."[1] . . . The student-narrator sketches a series of characters connected with the academy; some of these he clearly despises, while others seem to have left a distinctly favorable impression on his young mind. The predictably smooth, insidious headmaster is cleverly caricatured along with a prim, stuffy teacher of literature. But there are also sensitive portrayals: of a World War I veteran who suffers an emotional collapse as he looks at the young boys attending a Memorial Day assembly; and Laura Driscoll, a headstrong history teacher who dares to bring her subject to life for her students—and eventually gets fired for defending the anarchists Sacco and Vanzetti. At Driscoll's farewell appearance before students and faculty, the headmaster feigns sympathy for her, but she sees through him and retaliates: "Then Laura got up, called him a damned liar, swore down the length of the platform and walked out of the building" (174). If it didn't happen that way in real life, it should have. In the 1940s, as his style matured, this kind of twist would become a hallmark of Cheever's best work; conversely, it was the kind of dramatic touch that most of his Depression-era stories lack.

Cheever's most stinging rebukes are reserved for the story's ending, where he castigates the whole prep school nonethic: "As a college-preparatory school it was a fine school. In five years they could make raw material look like college material. They could clothe it and breed it and make it say the right things when the colleges asked it to talk. That was its duty" (174).

The young outcast finally broadens his attack to include the entire nation, whose values the school supposedly embodies, as well as its systemic need for self-delusion—a tendency that Cheever even then might have recognized as a hidden cause of the stock market crash of 1929: "Our country is the best country in the world. We are swimming in prosperity and our President is the best president in the world. We have larger apples and better cotton and faster and more beautiful machines. This makes us the greatest country in the world. Unemployment is a myth. Dissatisfaction is a fable. In preparatory school America is beautiful. It is the gem of the ocean and it is too bad. It is bad because people believe it all" (174).

The irony is somewhat heavy-handed, but when the former student looks back on his life at the academy and announces, "I have no school to go back to. I am not sorry. I am not at all glad" (174), the reader can understand his ambivalence. Because the story's viewpoint is so well defined, the narrative tone is clear and resonant—qualities that would not reemerge together in Cheever's style until he joined the army in World War II and started writing about military life. In 1930 Cheever at least thought he knew how American society worked, and his awareness made him righteously angry. His sense of how individuals and organizations operate for and against the common good, his intuitive awareness of the spiritual reality that lay behind the incidents of everyday life, his outrage at the fact that decency, goodness, and courage are not as powerful as the deadly machinery of industrial civilization—all of these are vividly alive in his first published story.

Cheever now had "proof" that he was a good storyteller when it came to using autobiographical material. But he could not yet be sure of either his stylistic or commercial range. As the impact of the Depression deepened and broadened, cynics were making themselves heard; and after a brief flirtation with impressionism, he made the understandable but damaging mistake of trying to sound like another Hemingway, or occasionally, Fitzgerald. Unfortunately he was a good imitator and persisted in the error, encouraged by the approval (starting in 1935) of the *New Yorker* and other magazines, until 1942.

What might be called Cheever's early naturalistic period got off to an odd beginning, with some experimental stories that are anything but naturalistic. In their rampant impressionism they suggest their writer's eagerness to break out of the strictly autobiographical mold, and in that light their shortcomings are almost commendable. "Fall River" was published in the autumn 1931 issue of *The Left*, a short-lived radical magazine; "Late Gathering" in the equally obscure *Pagany*. Both magazines represented a considerable falling off from the *New Republic*. And both tales are astonishing in their formlessness, following the accomplishments of "Expelled."

Because it skirts the edges of pro-Communist sentiment, "Fall River" is of some interest: it describes the disastrous effects of plant closings in New England and looks forward to the more impressive social commentary of "In Passing," a 1936 story. Primarily an experiment in mood creation, "Fall River" features painfully bleak descriptions of an industrial wasteland and is devoid of characterization. A brief excerpt from "Late Gathering" is perhaps more typical of both stories' preoccupation with rhetorical flourish at the expense of credibility. One of the female characters preciously scolds a young man, "You have never seen the fields as I have. You do not know what a flowered meadow is. You have never walked into fields that were blue and white and yellow and every flower as perfect as the nipples on your breast" (16).

To be fair, this is probably the sort of apprentice work Cheever was referring to in his preface to the 1978 collection of *Stories*, when he wrote: "A writer can be seen clumsily learning to walk, to tie his necktie, to make love, and to eat his peas off a fork. He appears much alone and determined to instruct himself. Naïve, provincial in my case, sometimes drunk, sometimes obtuse, almost always clumsy, even a selected display of one's early work will be a naked history of one's struggle to receive an education in economics and love" (vii). In neither of these stories does Cheever seem even remotely interested in creating a narrative structure that would lend coherence to his material. More than forty years later, in the twilight of his career, Cheever would still insist on the relative unimportance of plot or story line in his work: "I don't work with plots. I work with intuition, apprehension, dreams, concepts. Characters and events come simultaneously to me. . . . a good narrative is a rudimentary structure, rather like a kidney."[2]

But this approach to writing fiction is not without risk, as Cheever discovered. The four years following his initial success were more typical of the experience of young writers. Rejection replaced acceptance with a vengeance, and in all likelihood young John (or Jon, as he sometimes signed his stories) Cheever grew increasingly aware of the need to make his stories comprehensible—at least to magazine editors.

In 1935 Cheever returned to realism within structured story lines and finally "turned the corner" of commercial acceptance. Four of his stories appeared in the *New Yorker*. Thus he was able to demonstrate that "Expelled" had not been a fluke and that he could discipline himself to adhere to basic narrative conventions, perhaps even more closely than necessary. The stories are not exceptional, but they still offer informative glimpses of life during the Depression—a life whose rough edges Cheever knew intimately.

The following year he wrote a long story for the *Atlantic Monthly* that showed considerable promise. "In Passing" is a fairly thoughtful look at communism that might surprise readers familiar only with its author's postwar work.[3] Where "Fall River" hinted vaguely that the laborer who lived down the street might harbor radical ideas, this story puts all the red cards on the table. It combines two narrative strands, using a thematic connection that evolves from the viewpoint of a young man named Tom (one of Cheever's favorite names for characters with whom he seems to identify); and it is one of the few stories from this period written in the first person.

Tom is a free spirit lost in the wilderness of the Depression, here localized in a racetrack town that bears a close resemblance to Saratoga, New York. He is employed as a storeclerk by an emigré Jewish couple, who give him friendship as well as room and board. Through them he meets a genuine revolutionary named Girsdansky, who has left his home in eastern Europe to spread the gospel of communism in America. Girsdansky is a labor agitator, trying to foment social unrest by "educating" groups of supposedly discontented workers.

From the perspective of the late twentieth century, Girsdansky's zeal seems dated, but in the thirties he represented a "type" capable of striking real fear into the hearts of many Americans. The most important perspective from which to analyze him is not ours or theirs, of course, but Tom's. The story's protagonist is young but sophisticated enough to take the measure of Girsdansky. He sees that the revolutionary is skating on ice thin enough to bring down himself and those around him; still he follows him on his forays into local labor gatherings, drawn by curiosity and the visitor's intense commitment. The tension that drives the story is generated by the uncertainty of this relationship: will the radical convert the clerk? Cheever answers the question indirectly by establishing a clear contrast. Like Turgenev's anarchist Bazarov in *Fathers and Sons*, Girsdansky has a manner and appearance that command attention. He projects unusual inner strength and self-possession:

> He looked like the picture of Sir Galahad that used to hang in the Public Library of the town I come from.
>
> But after we had talked for a little while I knew he was older than that. He was at least in his early thirties. He did not talk like a boy, although his voice had the same clarity and callowness of his figure and his features. He talked like a man. The impression of youth that he gave was largely because he showed no trace of confusion or habit or vice. . . . (333)

Girsdansky repays Tom's admiration by revealing his most extreme views concerning the imminent decline of capitalism: "At first I thought it was something I should never see—or even my son. But now I feel sure I'll see it" (334). Tom listens attentively to these views, but his private comment to the reader reveals a great deal about both characters: "He talked like a book; his talk had the clarity and dryness of a book." Girsdansky departs for a tour of industrial cities, and after seeing him off Tom explores the raucous main street of the town, crowded with racetrack characters at the height of the season:

> the bar was full of touts and trainers and horsemen talking about horses. . . . Craps and roulette and chemin de fer tables were set up in a casino in the courtyard. I went down and watched the gaming for a little while and the faces above the tables. They were intent and greedy. The players were not rich. The betting was low, and some of the people, particularly some of the women, were shabbily dressed; but there was nothing in their faces but a love of money and the incorrigible dream of big money. (337)

Cheever stops short of analyzing this Dantean vision of lost souls, although he does have Tom liken the arriving crowds to "crippled pilgrims at the news of another miracle in Lourdes." The significance of the scene lies in its grimy vitality, a pulsating counterpoint to the dreariness that Girsdansky prefers to see when he arrives in this or any other town. What he has failed to understand is that most Americans are dreamers of a different school—and that this is both their curse and their deliverance. You may write a book about the tormented masses and call it *Girsdansky*, Cheever seems to say; you can even try to save those masses. But the instant you turn your back, they will be off to the casino, greedily pursuing their own idea of happiness. Or as Tom puts it: "Like the rest of the town, I bought dope and played the races, and on the last day Nicholas [his boss] gave me the afternoon off and I went down and saw Corabelle win the Hopeful" (337).

In the second part of the story, labor agitation and incipient communism give way to a more personal conflict involving Tom's family. The racing season ends, and Tom receives word from his father that the bank has foreclosed on their mortgage and sold their land. He returns home to find his parents unable to cope with their deteriorating situation. Their attempts to explain it alternate between absolute clarity and confused despair. Before the Depression they had been pros-

8

perous, but the good life has weakened their capacity for survival in bad times. Tom is not unsympathetic, especially toward his mother (she is not the man-devourer of Cheever's later fiction); for the most part, however, he depicts them in an oddly detached manner. If Girsdansky's extremism put his brand of politics outside Tom's sympathetic reach, at least he knew what he wanted. Tom's parents are merely pathetic in their grasping at financial straws: "'Did you get any long shots?' my father asked. 'I read in the paper that a sixty-to-one horse came in. I wondered if you had any money on her'" (338). Rather than staying and trying to help them fight in what looks like a hopeless cause, Tom decides to leave home again and try his luck in Boston. As he walks to the mall shortly after arriving there, he notices a small group gathered round a speaker. Almost predictably this turns out to be Girsdansky, proclaiming the eventual dictatorship of the proletariat. Tom turns away: "I don't know whether he recognized me or not. I walked down Charles Street scuffing up the dead leaves and wondering where I should be in another year" (343).

As with most of Cheever's Depression-era stories, the narrator gives us minimal interpretive guidance concerning the story's theme; he is the story's teller, and we are to draw our own conclusions. Has his father's hollow optimism seeped into Tom's consciousness, leading him to reject communism? A more plausible explanation can be found in the skepticism that sets the narrative tone of the entire story. Tom is uncertain of the future, just as the nation at large was uncertain in 1936. But he cannot trust a world vision that leaves so little room for the unruly, disreputable, greedy dreamers of Saratoga, or Boston, or Middle America. A revolutionary who "talks like a book," no matter how virtuous, stands little chance of success in an age when few people take themselves seriously as saints.

"In Passing" thus offers persuasive evidence that Cheever at twenty-four, while he was not yet the master of his craft, could be remarkably sensitive to the political realities of his time, and that he could see deeply into the recesses of the American soul. The fact that he speaks forthrightly, perhaps even autobiographically, of these things in the first person (although through a fictional creation) is also significant. Some readers might prefer that Tom follow Girsdansky's lead, but an intelligent reading should grant that his rejection of radicalism is deliberate and that Cheever has made it credible in human terms.

The story also demonstrates Cheever's determination not to let his earlier failed attempts at impressionistic writing dampen his enthusiasm for experiment. "In Passing" is actually the first of a group of five stories that use discontinuous dialogue to reveal or emphasize psychological stress; in this instance, Tom's parents slip in and out of disconnected, almost chaotic conversation in a manner reminiscent of that seen in some of the plays of Russian dramatist and short story writer Anton Chekhov. In Chekhov's *The Cherry Orchard*, for example, the Ranevsky family faces precisely the same financial and personal catastrophe as Tom's, and their disjointed conversations reflect their inner turmoil. It was actually during the period from 1936 to 1940 that Cheever started to earn the title later given him by John Leonard and other critics: "our Chekhov."[4]

Leonard was not referring specifically to disconnected dialogue in making the comparison, and there are other similarities between the *fiction* of Chekhov and that of Cheever that deserve exploration. But a careful reading of any of the stories in this "Chekhov set" (besides "In Passing," they include "Frère Jacques," 1938; "The Happiest Days," 1939; "It's Hot in Egypt," 1940; "I'm Going to Asia," 1940) will show that Cheever's use of the technique is essentially the same as the Russian master's. Although a direct line of influence between a particular play by Chekhov and a specific story by Cheever would be difficult to prove, there can be no doubt that at some point in his career Cheever "adopted" Chekhov as a literary idol. In the twilight of his life, when he was asked to deliver a lecture at Cornell as part of a special conference on Chekhov, he responded that he would be happy to do so for the price of carfare and a roof over his head.[5] The conclusion of his paper is particularly illuminating:

> What I remember most vividly of Chekhov is the last act, actually the last moments, of *Uncle Vanya*. The structure of the play is conventional enough although the cadence and penetration of the dialogue are Chekhov's . . . [there follows a plot summary]. The professor and his beauty have departed for Kharkov, where they will continue to be supported by Vanya's labor. Astrov has propositioned the beauty once more before she leaves. He remains ardent. He is refused. Now Vanya and Sonya, who helps him with the estate, watch Astrov pack before he leaves. These people possess none of the lures or attractions that will make love available to them. They are part of that population that must look for truth in simple, practical chores. The scene is one of sadness and despair. Then Astrov goes to the map on the wall and exclaims: *How hot it must be in Africa.*

This is a new note. This is the introduction of an abstraction.
This is for me the genius of Chekhov.[6]

The similarity between Astrov's remark and the title of Cheever's
"It's Hot in Egypt" is worth noting; even more to the point is the fact
that Cheever's experiments with conversational non sequiturs as a
means of conveying troubled states of mind are as controlled and effective as Chekhov's—and that the master was probably at the height
of his dramatic powers when he used the technique. If Chekhov the
dramatist did influence Cheever, of course, that is not surprising: the
young writer, in need of practical inspiration, may simply have turned
to one of the best creative artists and anatomists of middle-class life
ever to put pen to paper.

All of the stories in this group are fairly successful at delineating
interesting (and troubled) characters in difficult situations. "Frère
Jacques," however, stands out as the most intriguing and most dramatic. At the beginning of this story, a young woman returns to a rural
cabin with a package of supplies. She is greeted by a young man, apparently her husband, named Alex (we never learn her name). Alex
speaks with a Russian accent. We discover that they are preparing to
leave the cabin and move to "the city," apparently for financial reasons.
The young woman is clearly reluctant to leave; she strongly prefers
country life, so the decision to move is a source of friction.

But what is most unusual about the story, even for Cheever, is the
degree of ignorance that he inflicts on his readers concerning two key
points—and his use of discontinuous conversation to clarify them quite
late in the story. First, these young people are not married. This may
seem to be of minor significance, but its relation to the second, more
disturbing point increases its importance. In the midst of some idle
gossip about her shopping trip, the woman casually says, "And I
bought an ice cream for Heloise"—to which Alex responds, without
looking up from his newspaper, "You're telling me. It's all over her
face. Chocolate?"[7] At this point the reader may simply be confused,
because Baby Heloise hasn't been mentioned previously; or he may
decide that the couple has a child (and still be somewhat confused, but
fault Cheever's sloppy narrative technique). As it happpens, straightforward confusion is the proper response, but the second reading is also
partly correct. The narrator explains a few lines later that Heloise is
actually an inside joke of long standing between the couple. "She" is
an imaginary child that has taken the form of assorted packages and

bundles during the two years they have been together (perhaps coincidentally, but perhaps not, Chekhov has a minor character in *The Cherry Orchard* speak to an imaginary baby). As the story progresses, however, the joke becomes increasingly strained. The conversation continues, and it continues to refer to Heloise, while touching on topics that are as sensitive as an exposed nerve:

> "Oh, well," she said, "she's as tired as we, and we can't expect her to talk all the time. I do wish we could bring her up in the country, Alex. She'd be a brighter baby."
> "Money," he said. (380)

Money, or the lack of it—as in so many of Cheever's Depression-era stories—is an overriding concern for these young people. Their poverty forces them to leave the country for the city and prevents them from having a real child. A few moments later, as if to distract themselves from these inescapable facts, they slip into classic Chekhovian dialogue:

> "There's nothing more to do?" she asked.
> "No," he said. Her persistence in talking while he tried to read irritated him. "We can leave the keys here. We ought to get to bed soon. I want to start early in the morning. I'd like to get back to the city before dark."
> "That outboard sounds like a hornet," she said.
> The single sound above the chopping of the waves was the droning of an outboard, way up beyond Basin Bay.
> "What did you say about hornets?"
> "That outboard," she said, "it sounds like a hornet."
> "Oh," he said.
> "Want to go swimming?" she said. She stood with her back to him, looking out over the lake. She was still holding the laundry bundle. (380)

And a little later, still grasping the bundle, she spies a seagull (possibly another tip of Cheever's pen in Chekhov's direction), observing, "I'll bet they get homesick for the ocean." As the story ends, the couple's cheerfulness in the face of adversity has been completely eroded, revealing an underlying antagonism in a way that anticipates the dark revelations of "The Country Husband," "The Season of Divorce," and "The Brigadier and the Golf Widow."

Breakthroughs

In the late thirties and early forties, the world edged closer to war, and Cheever's short stories increasingly reflected the gradual shift in national mood from malaise to apprehensiveness. His work also continued to display an uncanny ability to discover the hidden significance in seemingly unpromising material—everything from childhood dancing class to racetrack romance. In the two years before the United States entered the war, he published twenty-seven stories, making this his most prolific period in terms of number of stories produced. His marriage to Mary Winternitz in March of 1941 may have had something to do with this, and with his turning out to be more self-assured as a writer after he entered the service.

With few exceptions, the stories Cheever published between 1935 and early 1942 are coldly detached in tone, as if the teller were curious about his characters and their problems—but nothing more. They are essentially naturalistic reports on biological specimens responding to various stimuli, rather than stories about people told by someone with a human interest in their human spirits. As such they are technically impressive, and magazines like the *New Yorker* were quick to realize that young Cheever's eye for revealing details was as sharp as that of any of its more established writers. Still, readers familiar with his work of the late forties onward, starting with "The Enormous Radio," will sense that something is missing in these earlier stories. The passionate voice of "Expelled" had been muffled, or at least toughened into a flat monotone.

The war would give that voice a deeper modulation and make it more assertive. About three weeks before Cheever was inducted into the army, the *New Yorker* (18 April 1942) published "The Shape of a Night,"[8] a story that marks a clear transition from the Depression into the war period for Cheever. The central characters are a New York office worker named Tom and his wife Marian. They are waiting out the final days before American involvement in the conflict, and their conversation is typically "tough" but also tinged with melancholy, revealing a weariness with a world so intolerant of youthful happiness.

They are visited by another young woman, Helen, whose husband is already in the service. When she learns that Tom will soon join the army, she loses control: "They'll kill all our men. We're lost" (152). Tom calms her by offering a cigarette, and after she leaves, he and Marian go to bed. While Marian sleeps, Tom—little more than a sounding board up to this point in the narrative—considers the unkind fate meted out to his generation:

> The girls Tom met then used to say things like that. "My older sister went abroad three times. We used to have five servants. We used to have four cars. Mother used to play bridge at ten cents a point, but after the crash . . . " They were a generation with more responsibilities than some, and whatever normal life they had been able to find had been stolen. . . . they had been told repeatedly that the spurious peace they lived in would not outlast their youth, and they were late to see that it was over. (154)

That kind of introspection in a main character had not been seen in Cheever's work since "Expelled." It represents a return to the kind of personal and artistic confidence that had heralded his introduction to American letters twelve years before. By the time he wrote "The Shape of a Night," his emotional identification with the young men and women he presumes to speak for (and the equating of Cheever's viewpoint with his narrator's can be justified in this case) was too strong to be contained or masked, and it makes the story better than it would be otherwise. They had suffered in the wilderness of the Depression, and so had he. The question of whether Cheever is Tom, and Mary is Marian, is finally irrelevant.

But point of view in a story is crucial, if we accept the notion that most storytellers "have something to say" about their narrative material to their readers—an assumption by no means universally accepted, but essential to an understanding of Cheever's apprenticeship. Cheever himself apparently called that idea into question in a few of his early tales—at some cost to his professional progress. Once he had come to terms with the need for clear expression, however, it was only a matter of time until the strong will first asserted in "Expelled" started to resurface.

Surprisingly, given the cynicism of the Depression stories, this reassertion took the form of a tempered patriotism in Cheever's published work from 1942 to 1945. As an enlisted man in the army, Cheever spent several months in training as an infantryman before being transferred to the Signal Corps. Stories like "Sergeant Limeburner" and "The Invisible Ship" (there were a dozen in all) offer vivid depictions of life in barracks and training situations, as it was lived by men from all parts of the country and all walks of life. The situations range from comic to brutally tragic, but in almost every case, the narrator's admiration for his fellow soldiers is evident. Some of these men are foolish, and others border on the criminal in their behavior; but for the most part they take their new identity as soldiers seriously and treat each other with simple decency.

In "The Invisible Ship,"[9] for instance, a Midwesterner named Nelson is about to be sent home after being judged too old for service, only to discover that his wallet has been stolen. His barracks mates, rather than showing their jealousy at his early departure, collect enough money to pay for his trip. In a series of letters to his wife written not long before the story appeared, Cheever tells her of just such an occurrence happening in his company.[10] The actual incident involved his company commander's restricting the entire unit to their quarters, then lifting the restriction shortly afterward, although the thief was not discovered. Unlike his commander, however, Cheever couldn't let the matter drop; the storytelling impulse had been triggered.

In a literary sense the actual story must have looked unfinished to Cheever. To satisfy the demands of formal narrative, he created a small "cast" of enlisted men surrounding the victim, a Midwesterner renamed Algot Larssen, and introduced a second conflict to the moral issue raised by the theft. This comes in the shape of "Captain Beaumont," the fictional company commander, who assumes responsibility for bringing the culprit to justice. Beaumont is described as too "nervous and abrupt" for his position: "Decisiveness was a characteristic he admired, and he would sooner make a quick decision than a judicious one" (17). Beaumont demonstrates this trait by selecting three men with questionable records for interrogation. Ironically one of them eventually turns out to be guilty, but in the meantime the captain proves his incompetence by accusing all three in turn, trying to force a confession. When this fails, it remains for the enlisted men to solve the mystery and dispense their own rough form of justice.

Before that happens, Beaumont gives a stagy lecture to the assembled company and puts the unit under "quarantine" (in one of his letters to Mary, Cheever reported that his commander had compared stealing to a contagious disease like the mumps). A crap game played

15

in the hothouse atmosphere of the restriction to quarters brings out the truth. One of the GIs has an unusually large stake, and an exchange of insults establishes his guilt. A bloody fight ensues, but the money is finally returned to Larssen; the basic decency of the men is then reasserted in a burst of comradeship:

> MacInty put his arm over Larssen's shoulder and walked over to his bed. "Now when you have a drink in Minneapolis you can have a drink for us," he said. He sat down beside Larssen.
>
> "I'm going to miss all you fellows," Larssen said weakly. "I don't want to go away only it's just I'm not so young. Such fine fellows I never met before in all my life. Such fine fellows. I would like to go to war with you. You will win the war. . . ." (21)

As it turned out, unfortunately, the unit Cheever trained with before being transferred to the Signal Corps was badly mauled in the invasion of France. Although this story's premise is certifiably realistic and unpleasant, Cheever's point is not how awful it is that in a large group of men, drawn from all levels of American society, one should prove to be a criminal. On the contrary, the story emphasizes the moral sense and simple decency of most of the GIs, who take it on themselves to "right" the wrong done to someone luckier than themselves.

The younger Cheever of the thirties might well have chosen to pattern the events of the story more closely on the events that inspired it, since major changes would distort reality. It seems unlikely that Cheever's army experience had transformed him into a sentimental patriot; still, the alteration in the story's outcome suggests that the significant transition in his personal viewpoint noted in "The Shape of a Night" was being carried forward. In this instance, although the narrative voice is more muted, the sequence of events (modified to create a more satisfying conclusion than reality afforded) suggests a more assertive shaping consciousness; Cheever the technician is becoming Cheever the artist in khaki. He never distinguished himself as a soldier (now in his thirties, he was past his physical prime), but he was starting to come into his own as a writer.

One of the final stories in the wartime series, "Manila" (*New Yorker*, 28 July 1945), is set in the Philippine capital during the mopping up operations following the return of General Douglas MacArthur earlier that year. Cheever's army discharge tersely notes that he was on "sea duty" from 11 April to 15 June, and it is safe to assume that he was in Manila during May. Some of his friends from the forties[11] knew that he had been assigned to a Signal Corps project there but are not able to recall his having discussed it with them. On the admittedly insufficient evidence of this story and one other ("Love in the Islands," *New Yorker,* 7 December 1946) as well as the discharge, it seems clear that although he did not see combat, he saw its aftermath.

"Manila" follows the misadventures of Chester Schmidt, an ordinary soldier from Pennsylvania obsessed with souvenir hunting. To him, the ruined city and its environs look like an ideal place to indulge that desire. Cheever describes the bombed-out neighborhoods from Chester's viewpoint: "The streets of the city were littered with Japanese centavo notes, and Chester stuffed his pockets with them. He looked at the ruins with the unsentimental curiosity of a tourist."[12]

Like too many soldiers in wartime, Chester is so preoccupied with his souvenir-chasing (a desire that in some cases cannot be explained by mere greed) that he fits a stereotype that had yet to be formulated: the ugly American. His chief goal is to find or buy a hara-kiri knife or samurai sword, and when he hears that a local family may own such a weapon, he jumps at the chance to visit them. On meeting the Hernandez family, who are markedly genteel by contrast, he immediately betrays his own vulgarity:

> "I will not sell the knife," Mr. Hernandez said.
> "Well, you won't get no more than a hundred pesos," Chester said crossly. (22)

Then in a passage that looks forward to similar moments in his more mature work (they can be called epiphanies, in James Joyce's sense of "intense revelations"), Cheever gives Chester a chance to redeem himself through self-discovery. Later the same day Mr. Hernandez's daughter appears at Chester's camp and presents him with the knife (actually an Indian weapon), insisting that it be taken as a gift when Chester, at first confused, refuses to pay for it. To remove any doubt that the soldier is deeply affected by this act of generosity and gratitude, Cheever ends the story with a scene in which Chester, leaving his chowline at the end of the day, notices a Filipino mother and child standing at the edge of the camp. The child, afflicted with a hacking cough, is crying.

> "I guess your baby would like to get some milk into him, wouldn't he, now?" Chester said. He handed her his cup and spoon, and she smiled and sat on a stump and began to feed the child with the

17

spoon. . . . Chester watched the feeding himself and, as he
watched, he shivered violently and unaccountably. His mother
would have said that someone had walked across his grave. Then he
thought he was going to cry. (23)

Because he avoids any mention of the Hernandez incident here,
Cheever makes Chester's actions appear almost instinctive, but the
connection is clear: these are the only two developed incidents in the
story. This combination of moral inference and positive theme is almost without precedent in his early stories.[13]

As in "The Invisible Ship," Cheever in this instance comes close to
idealizing the common GI; he actually takes the process further than
he had in most of the earlier wartime stories. Chester Schmidt is one
of only a few soldiers drawn by Cheever that grow substantially as characters, becoming more human than they were when their stories
began.

A more assertive narrative presence can be seen in most of Cheever's
stories from this period, but because none of them are directly concerned with combat, his wartime work lacks the inherent interest of
stories by Irwin Shaw, James Jones, and others. When the war ended,
Cheever wrote a series of six narratives about the problems of veterans
and their spouses making the readjustment to civilian life. The "Town
House" series—in part autobiographical, according to Cheever's friend
John Weaver[14]—reports the troubled relationships of several such couples forced to live together because of the postwar housing shortage in
New York. If the physical circumstances are vastly different, the personal strengths and shortcomings of the young marrieds in this series
are quite similar to those found in both the city-based and suburban
stories that would follow.

But there is virtually no precedent for the most widely read of
Cheever's short stories, a fantastic tale set in a Manhattan apartment.
It would be only a slight exaggeration, in fact, to claim that the apartment building in "The Enormous Radio" (1947)[15] is a central character
in the story; it is as alive as any of the "real" people in the narrative.
The animation of inanimate structures is an ancient literary device, and
such writers as Émile Zola had fully explored the thematic possibilities
inherent in the technique long before Cheever tried it. Few writers,
however, have been able to achieve the intensity of effect that Cheever
creates with seeming ease in "The Enormous Radio" by blending realism, fantasy, comedy, and pathos. By carefully manipulating these

elements into a structure that is larger than the sum of its parts, Cheever first hypnotizes the reader and then illuminates some of the darker regions of the human psyche.

The story's two main characters, Jim and Irene Westcott, are described in the opening lines as "the kind of people who seem to strike that satisfactory average of income, endeavor, and respectability that is reached by the statistical reports in college alumni bulletins" (33). They are outwardly as normal as can be: productive, law-abiding, the parents of two young children. The teller of the story merely hints at a skeptical view of their life-style (Cheever may even be parodying himself) when he records that the Westcotts go to the theater "on an average of 10.3 times a year" (33).

The only significant difference between the Westcotts and other young couples in their set is their interest in serious music. When their old radio suddenly dies in the middle of a Schubert quartet, Jim decides to buy a replacement. This could serve as the stuff of comedy pure and simple, and in fact Cheever would work on scripts for the *Life with Father* television series only a few years later. A less experienced writer might have succumbed to the comic potential of his narrative premise, but Cheever had other intentions.

The Westcotts soon discover that their new radio can garner sounds and conversations from every corner of their building. At first the narrator suggests that this is due to some technical oddity in the radio or the building itself, but it quickly becomes apparent that no "logical" explanation will suffice. The radio tunes in quite accurately on the private lives of the building's tenants. The Westcotts eavesdrop on "a monologue on salmon fishing in Canada, a bridge game, running comments on home movies of what had apparently been a fortnight at Sea Island, and a bitter family quarrel about an overdraft at the bank" (37). For awhile this incredible addition to their home strikes the Westcotts as funny, a source of free entertainment beyond their wildest imagining. But the reference to a family quarrel should warn the reader that the story is not simply a comic sketch. The radio takes on tremendous symbolic importance when we realize that the particular form of voyeurism the Westcotts have succumbed to is essentially no different from the "normal" reader's own, supposedly more respectable vice: looking over the narrator's shoulder into the turmoil of his characters' lives. In this light Cheever, or any good storyteller, is our enormous radio, and by extension we are the Westcotts.

Thus "The Enormous Radio" converts a comic premise into a powerfully enlightening narrative engine. In one brilliant stroke, Cheever had both fully exploited and utterly transcended his own cleverness. More than forty years later the idea seems so obvious, and the writing so effortless, that it is easy for us to make the same mistake that some of Cheever's contemporaries made by overlooking the great advance this story represents for its writer and, I think, for the short story as a narrative form. It is an amazingly compact blend of fantasy and stark realism. In the following excerpt, for example, Cheever manages to move Irene from a restaurant back to her apartment, establish the almost magnetic hold of the radio on her consciousness, reinforce the terrible truthfulness of the radio, and advance the theme of pervasive, inescapable duplicity:

> Irene had two Martinis at lunch, and she looked searchingly at her friend and wondered what her secrets were. They had intended to go shopping after lunch, but Irene excused herself and went home. She told the maid she was not to be disturbed; then she went into the living room, closed the doors, and switched on the radio. She heard, in the course of the afternoon, the halting conversation of a woman entertaining her aunt, the hysterical conclusion of a luncheon party, and a hostess briefing her maid about some cocktail guests. "Don't give the best Scotch to anyone who hasn't white hair," the hostess said. "See if you can get rid of that liver paste before you pass those hot things, and could you lend me five dollars? I want to tip the elevator man." (38)

T. S. Eliot has noted that humankind cannot bear too much reality, but Cheever seems determined to give us a strong dose of it; not the least disturbing aspect of "reality" in this case is the obsessive need of the Westcotts to hear it in such a sneaky fashion.

Cheever had achieved economy of style after his first few stories, but he had rarely demonstrated this kind of smooth, assured balance even in his army stories. Having released himself from his addiction to realism, he was clearly enjoying the full exercise of his talent. How many of his readers had at some time or other wanted to spy on their neighbors? Having drawn them in this far, he could now compel them to overhear an eclectic catalog of human folly, by turns humorous and frightening. We finally share in the psychic pain of the Westcotts when, too late, they realize they have heard too much:

"Of course we're happy," he said tiredly. He began to surrender his
resentment. "Of course we're happy. I'll have that damned radio
fixed or taken away tomorrow." He stroked her soft hair. "My poor
girl," he said.
"You love me, don't you?" she asked. "And we're not hypercrit-
ical or worried about money or dishonest, are we?"
"No, darling," he said. (40)

But the following day, after the radio has been "fixed" and dutifully
tunes in classical music, the Westcotts have a terrible argument—about
their own problems with money and dishonesty—as the radio news
reports disasters from around the globe. In a masterful demonstration
of his storytelling art, Cheever has quietly yanked us out of our fasci-
nation with his clever story into an awareness of what we should have
known all along: all those Westcotts parading up and down the super-
market aisles of America are every bit as normal and abnormal as we
are. The story needs no explicitly stated moral; awareness is the beginning of understanding and sympathy for our fellow humans, and in
that direction, Cheever knew, lies salvation.

"Roseheath" is a startling contrast to "The Enormous Radio." Because the *New Yorker* has traditionally held back publication of some
pieces for seasonal and other reasons, it is impossible to date the writing of these stories, but "Roseheath" appeared in mid-August, three
months after "The Enormous Radio" and two weeks after a more pro-
saic (and more seasonal) tale called "The Common Day."[16] "Roseheath" is one of the funniest pieces Cheever ever wrote. In a few of
the stories from the thirties and earlier forties he had hinted at an interest in comic twists of plot and dialogue, but with few exceptions
these were rarely indulged in, the business of a realist having to do
with loftier purposes than amusement. One point of similarity between
this and "The Enormous Radio" is found in Cheever's deceptively
bland beginning; one suspects that he had come to know his *New
Yorker* readers by this stage of his career and derived a mischievous
pleasure from surprising them. In this case however, in the manner of
O. Henry, he maintains the deception until nearer the story's end.

"Roseheath" has no serious point to make, though for its author it
represented a serious break with the past. The sense of playfulness
found in much of Cheever's best work of the fifties and sixties is given
full expression for the first time in this story. It is also prototypical in

that its two main characters, the Wilcoxes, are the first of Cheever's postwar suburbanites.

Ethel and Dana Wilcox are a young married couple cheated by time and circumstance (or so they feel) out of a particular happiness. A neighborhood home where Ethel had spent many pleasant afternoons as a young girl swimming and playing tennis has been sold, and is presumably lost to the Wilcoxes forever. A short distance into the story, however, they are delighted to meet the Fields, who have just bought the home, and to find that they seem quite conventional. The family consists of an older couple, their son, and daughter-in-law.

Naturally enough, when they are invited to the Fields' for a swimming party, the Wilcoxes are overjoyed. To this point the only hint Cheever has offered that something unusual is afoot appears when Dana meets Mr. Field's son, Roger, at the train station one morning and learns more about the family than he had expected: "'I go in to the city only three days a week now,' Roger said. 'I'm not working. I'm being analyzed. We've all been analyzed. That is, everyone but my wife. . . . Mother's been analyzed twice. She plays the violin now'" (29). Roger also informs Dana that the Fields have moved East to follow their psychoanalyst. But Dana is not the most perceptive of men, and he fails to sense the potential for trouble ahead. The Wilcoxes arrive at the Fields' on the appointed afternoon and join their hosts at poolside. There follows some amiable chit-chat, the point of which seems to be everyone's relief at finding everyone else so agreeable. Then without warning Mr. Fields takes off his shorts and prepares to dive into the pool.

Instead of immediately registering the Wilcoxes' shock or dismay, Cheever is content to have Mrs. Field observe that the pool water was changed the previous day, in spite of a local water shortage, because she "can't stand a warm pool." Only then do we find out that Ellen realizes her eagerness to reclaim the past has backfired:

> "The Heywoods used to feel that way," Ethel said. Her voice was strained. "Mrs. Heywood used to say," she went on nervously, shrilly, conscious of the naked man at her side, "Mrs. Heywood used to say that she'd rather have her garden wither than swim in tepid water." (30)

Ellen struggles to keep her composure as one after another, the Fields enter the pool undressed. But when Dana decides to follow their example, she suddenly remembers a dinner engagement. The story ends wistfully, moments before their departure: "Ethel massaged her face, so that her smile would appear natural when she said goodbye to the Fields—goodbye and thank you and goodbye to Roseheath forever" (31).

The story material is somewhat less fantastic than that of its predecessor, and Cheever is here more interested in comic effects achieved through understatement than he had been in "The Enormous Radio." But once again his concern with accurate depiction of human behavior—especially Ellen's inner turmoil, in this case—is very evident. Ellen has done nothing wrong, yet to the extent that acute embarrassment can be a form of suffering, she suffers. The question of whether she is too prudish for her own good is not strictly relevant. Cheever's disdain for psychoanalysis and its results has now been established,[17] and the fact that our final focus in the story is on Ellen's position suggests that we should sympathize with her. The situation loses none of its humor if we do.

In stark contrast, this final narrative in the breakthrough trilogy, "Torch Song," is one of the most oppressively unfunny tales Cheever produced.[18] It appeared almost two months later, in October of 1947, and was followed by a string of more conventional stories, all of them appearing in the *New Yorker*. (From mid-1948 to late 1949 Cheever published only twice and was probably working on a novel.) "Torch Song" is also quite long and almost invites the kind of misunderstanding that could do considerable damage to Cheever's reputation as an original storyteller. The potential for such misunderstanding centers on one of its two main characters, the unfortunate, ghoulish Joan Harris—a woman who redirects the evil that has befallen her onto a long line of even more unfortunate men. One of these is the other main character and the story's protagonist, Jack Lorey.

Once again the story's plot is patiently developed, so that only toward the end can the reader grasp the full significance of what he has read, something the narrator has clearly known from the beginning: Joan is a ghoulish creature, who lives by feeding on the death agonies of men. The delayed triggering of that realization is quite remarkable given the length and general coherence of the story, and can be explained by noting that in several of her relationships, as chronicled by Jack, she appears to be more victim than victimizer. Initially we imagine that Jack follows Joan's progress, such as it is, because he is "fond" of her, the two of them having come to New York from the same town in Ohio. But as their paths cross and recross, and as each meeting yields another story of horror, it becomes inevitable that Jack—whose own marriages and divorces are scarcely reported—will eventually have more than a passing interest in her, and she in him:

> In the darkness, Joan began to talk about her departed lovers, and from what she said Jack gathered that they had all had a hard time. Nils, the suspect count, was dead. Hugh Bascomb, the drunk, had joined the Merchant Marine and was missing in the North Atlantic. Franz, the German, had taken poison the night the Nazis bombed Warsaw. "We listened to the news on the radio," Joan said, "and then he went back to his hotel and took poison." (98–99)

Bald recitation of the story's "facts," however, lends itself to the false notion that this is an exercise in misogyny. Nowhere does Cheever state or suggest that Joan consciously seeks out men to destroy. She takes them as she finds them, and if anything, it is her passivity that seems to draw out the worst in them. In fact, by the time he finally glides into a deeper connection with her, Jack has made a thorough mess of his life, and Joan has had nothing to do with that. She is no diabolical sorceress, although Jack implies as much when, having fallen seriously ill himself, he finally comprehends the morbidity of her existence: "'Does it make you feel young to watch the dying?' he shouted. 'Is that the lewdness that keeps you young? Is that why you dress like a crow? Oh, I know there's nothing I can say that will hurt you'" (102).

Following the outburst that sends Joan away, Jack pulls himself together and moves out of the apartment in which Joan had threatened to nurse him through his illness, presumably to start a new life. And there the story ends, so it might appear that his assessment should be the reader's, and a feeling of relief after suffering does seem appropriate. But if Joan is not a witch or diabolical force, what does the story mean?

I would suggest that Cheever removed the idea of deliberate evil from his portrayal of Joan for a thematic reason. He chose not to oversimplify her, I suspect, in order to drive home the point that evil does not depend on human volition for its existence. Its origins are so ancient and its lineage so tangled that it lives in the marrow of saint, sinner, and ordinary mortal alike. And what is an ordinary mortal after all but some combination of saint and sinner? If Jack is both, so must

Joan be. For a conventional moralist this may be a repellent notion, but for Cheever it essentially means that an ostensibly good behavior (nursing someone who is ill) can in a given context be a serious perversion, and vice versa. "Torch Song" disturbs us precisely because it refuses to simplify the moral universe.

An attempt to locate a crucial "moment"—even one extending over several months—in John Cheever's fifty-two-year career may in itself seem simplistic. As we have seen, the pivotal year of 1947 was strenuously prepared for by Cheever: first, with a protracted apprenticeship extending from 1930 to 1942, and subsequently by a dramatic maturing that occurred after his marriage and during his army service from 1942 to 1946. In this light Cheever's flowering forth as an imaginative, even brilliant writer of short stories might almost appear inevitable. It was anything but that. Cheever was taking a professional risk, and it is to the credit of his editor William Maxwell and the *New Yorker* that they were willing to accept such unusual new material, albeit from an established performer.

Whether or not Cheever had read Struthers Burt's prediction of future success for him (see "The Critics"), it seems clear that early in 1947, following his military service, he became determined to impose a higher order of reality—what is usually referred to as fantasy—on his story material. Hitherto that material had been largely the stuff of life as he observed it during the Depression and the war years, selected and reassembled to serve as good naturalistic realism in fiction. But with the appearance of "The Enormous Radio," "Roseheath," and "Torch Song" he showed that he was capable of drawing on a much greater imaginative range, and determined to do so. While he is not an intrusive presence in these stories, it is obvious in each of them that behind the prism of observation there is an informed intelligence sorting out events, a critical eye analyzing and connecting details, an architect building sophisticated themes into the story's structure.

In "The Enormous Radio" he ventured into something approaching existential awareness and raised serious ethical questions about the meaning of personal involvement and self-delusion in the lives of his characters—people disturbingly like those who stare out at us from behind the bathroom mirror every morning. In "Roseheath" he finally gave full rein to an impish sense of humor that he had deliberately suppressed in his earlier work. He also managed to evoke sympathy for the victim of his comic situation, by carefully establishing the absurdity of its perpetrators. And in "Torch Song" he turned his hand to full-blown, macabre fantasy reminiscent of Poe, skillfully describing the pathology of a poisonous relationship that takes years to develop, then ripens and dies overnight. In this case his depiction of his principal female character can be criticized as primitive, but it is much fuller than that given her near-victim and far from stereotypical. As with "The Enormous Radio," any attempt to "solve" the story is simply inappropriate. In fact, all three stories seem more concerned with narrative possibilities than neat solutions. In the flowering of time those possibilities would again branch out and bear such diverse, remarkable fruit as "Goodbye, My Brother," "The Country Husband," "The Housebreaker of Shady Hill," and "The Swimmer."

Thus 1947 can be seen as a watershed year for John Cheever. The younger Cheever of the 1930s had not demonstrated much interest in such possibilities, although as an aspiring writer and occasional critic[19] he was constantly faced with questions of narrative technique. Cheever the thirty-five-year-old husband, father, and ex-soldier was ready to resolve them for himself, and if a period of self-doubt followed because the world had not quite understood, that was only natural. In the long run, the risk proved worth the taking.

New Directions

Compared to the prolific period of the early forties, the last two years of the decade were relatively dry ones for Cheever in terms of both published writing and attempts at setting new directions for himself. The technical facility displayed in such stories as "The Summer Farmer" (1948), "Vega" (1949), and later "The Season of Divorce" (1950) would suggest that Cheever's skills were as sharp as ever, if not more finely honed. He had yet to fulfill his goal of publishing a novel, however, and it seems probable that he was at work on his first longer work—possibly an early version of *The Wapshot Chronicle*—during these years.

The Cheevers had not yet moved to the New York suburbs, and most of the stories from this period are city-based. "Christmas Is a Sad Season for the Poor" (1949), for example, is reminiscent of "The Enormous Radio" in its use of an apartment building elevator operator as a device to bring together several characters in a single narrative strand wrapped around the theme of duplicity—in this case at Christmastime. It is less successful, however, because Cheever fails to achieve a satisfactory balance between serious and comic elements in his material. By turns the story seems to applaud the efforts of Charlie, the elevator man, to con tenants out of gifts that he later shares with a poor family, and to mock the futility of his gesture when those gifts are mindlessly passed on to another poor family.

A more interesting and more enigmatic story appeared the following year. "The Season of Divorce"[20] is representative of a sizable group of Cheever narratives exploring marital strife, a subject that held his attention more consistently than any other throughout his career. The fact that the Cheevers' own marriage was at times troubled by internal and external pressures may have some bearing on this, but it would be a mistake to read these stories as essentially autobiographical. Cheever himself complained about the tendency to reduce fiction to a simple retelling of the author's life experience,[21] and he certainly would have seen enough other couples experiencing matrimonial difficulty to supply his imagination with the material it needed to produce insightful fiction on the subject.

In "The Season of Divorce" that imaginative element appears to play a major role. Starting with the commonplace that married women do not cease to be attractive to men other than their husbands, Cheever builds a credible case for a wife's being pursued by a physician named Trencher. The doctor makes his affection blatantly obvious not only to her but to her husband, the story's narrator. Cheever invests the narrator's wife, Ethel, with the same generosity of spirit that characterizes Robert Browning's murder victim in "My Last Duchess"; the storyteller in this case is not inclined to kill his wife, but he is certainly jealous and infuriated by Dr. Trencher's persistence in the face of his equally apparent anger. The doctor goes as far as to deliver roses to Ethel personally, an event that sparks a heated exchange between husband and wife. Up to this point Ethel has been depicted as a fairly limited character, absorbed in her familial responsibilities until the advent of Trencher, whose advances she hesitates to discourage. During the argument it becomes clear that in fact she is multidimensional and that some of her attitudes are firmly grounded on resentment:

> In the bare kitchen light, meant for peeling potatoes and washing dishes, she looked very tired.
> "Will the children be able to go out tomorrow?"
> "Oh, I hope so," she said. "Do you realize that I haven't been out of this apartment in over two weeks?" She spoke bitterly and this startled me. (142)

Later, as their confrontation winds down to a roadblock of noncommunication, Ethel delivers a convincing statement of her frustration—a statement that Cheever himself may not have subscribed to, but that he deserves credit for including if we recall that the story predates by many years the women's liberation movement of the seventies:

> "In Grenoble," she said, "I wrote a long paper on Charles Stuart in French. A professor at the University of Chicago wrote me a letter. I couldn't read a French newspaper without a dictionary today, I don't have the time to follow the newspaper, and I am ashamed of my incompetence, ashamed of the way I look. Oh, I guess I love you, I do love the children, but I love myself, I love my life, it has some value and some promise for me and Trencher's roses make me

feel that I'm losing this, that I'm losing my self-respect. Do you
know what I mean, do you understand what I mean?" (143)

Unfortunately but realistically he doesn't understand, and the story
tapers off to a fairly safe, subdued ending after the narrator chases
Trencher from their apartment by tossing a potted geranium at him.
But at least Cheever refuses to paint Ethel as dutifully overjoyed at
her husband's heroic banishment of the interloper. Although this conclusion will fail to satisfy those who would like to see a clearing of the
air between husband and wife, it does sound that note of wistful ambiguity that would soon become a hallmark of Cheever's stories about
troubled marriages. This alliance will survive, it suggests, but only as
a shadow of what it had been, with Ethel fulfilling her responsibilities
to her husband and children as if in a daze: "she feeds them, bathes
them, and sets the table, and stands for a moment in the middle of the
room, trying to make some connection between the evening and the
day. Then it is over. She lights the four candles, and we sit down to
our supper" (146).

Thus a reader with more traditional values can find in "The Season
of Divorce" a vindication of the idea that the sanctity of the home
should be preserved at all costs, while a more liberal interpretation
would refer to the melancholy tone of the story's coda as proof that
Cheever's intent is to argue for Ethel's perspective. It strains credulity
to think that Cheever wanted to have it both ways, and thus the
enigma. But it may be unfair to fault Cheever for not taking sides in
this case; for him to present Ethel's perspective—and not just her husband's—with clarity and sympathy is an accomplishment that he would
not often replicate.

A different kind of ambiguity pervades "Goodbye, My Brother"
(1951),[22] a story in which Cheever breaks new ground and explores a
theme that clearly absorbed a great deal of his psychic energy. Once
again the subject matter is inherently difficult, and the moral question
it raises is exceptionally complex. But this time the story's resolution
of the issues it raises is very decisive. In this retelling of the biblical
Cain and Abel conflict, good and evil are not always easy to separate,
and the "bad" brother is actually the victim of violence.

The story is set at "Laud's Head . . . on the shore of one of the
Massachusetts islands" (3), more specifically at a beachfront house
owned by the Pommeroy family, its central focus. Its true location,

however, is that border area of the New England spirit that Nathaniel Hawthorne so expertly delineated in stories like "The Maypole of Marymount" a century before Cheever attempted his own exploration: the mysterious terrain where Puritan moralist confronts Anglican free thinker in a conflict of opposed wills.

The narrator is one of four grown Pommeroy children who periodically gather at the home with their widowed mother. Three of these siblings—the narrator, his sister Diana, and brother Chaddy—enjoy each other's company and their mother's; the problem is with Lawrence, or "Tifty." (As he often does, Cheever hints at what is to come by having the narrator recall Lawrence's two other nicknames, "Little Jesus" and "the Croaker.") Lawrence's chief characteristic emerges shortly into the story, when all of the adults assemble for cocktails on the terrace "so that we could see the bluffs and the sea and the islands in the east" (5). Their mother offers Lawrence a Martini, and he gruffly asks for some rum instead. The request annoys Mrs. Pommeroy because she considers rum a poor choice and because there is none available. Building on this seemingly minor point, Cheever proceeds to establish the story's central conflict. (Social drinking—often to excess—becomes a pervasive feature in Cheever's fiction starting in the early fifties and continuing until his hospitalization for alcoholism in 1976. In some stories, but surprisingly few, he seems to connect excessive drinking and the psychological problems of his characters.)

Lawrence's disagreeableness, seemingly trivial at first, actually points to a deeper flaw in his character: he invariably tends to search out and fix on the most unpleasant or disturbing aspect of any situation, social or otherwise. When Diana is escorted from the house by an admirer she has met in France, Lawrence stuns the rest of the family by asking, "Is that the one she's sleeping with now?" (6). The narrator records his mother's dismay at this and then analyzes his brother's offensiveness in light of his ancestry:

> The branch of the Pommeroys to which we belong was founded by a minister who was eulogized by Cotton Mather for his untiring abjuration of the Devil. The Pommeroys were ministers until the middle of the nineteenth century, and the harshness of their thought—man is full of misery, and all earthly beauty is lustful and corrupt—has been preserved in books and sermons. The temper of our family changed somewhat and became more lighthearted, but when I was of school age, I can remember a cousinage of old men

and women who seemed to hark back to the dark days of the ministry and to be animated by perpetual guilt and the deification of
the scourge. (6)

This goes directly to the heart of the conflict between the narrator and
his brother.

Similarly, the dead weight of a Calvinist heritage figured heavily in
Cheever's own upbringing. In a 1978 interview with Cheever John
Hersey quoted this section of "Goodbye, My Brother" and asked him
if it described his own family. Cheever's response was guarded but
candid. "Yes, it does. Of course I am describing a character in fiction,
and any confusion between autobiography and fiction is lamentable.
The darkness—the capacity for darkness that was cherished by New
England—certainly colored our lives."[23] And beyond question, the
theme of Puritan-style guilt and mortification informs many of Cheever's better stories, among them "The Enormous Radio," "The Lowboy," and "The Swimmer." But nowhere is it more crucial to a story's
unfolding than in "Goodbye, My Brother," where it is the key to Lawrence's personality and the main cause of his unexpected downfall.

When Mrs. Pommeroy tries to describe planned improvements in
the property, Lawrence predicts that the house will slip into the sea in
a few years. While the rest of the family plays tennis, he inspects the
home for evidence of his dead father's foolish addiction to the past. A
sizable portion of the home has been laboriously "antiqued"; Tifty
sees this as a failure to confront the realities of the present. But from
the narrator's perspective, his brother's failure to find any saving grace
in the present is his most odious quality, a sin that will eventually merit
severe retribution.

To overcome their animus toward Lawrence, the other Pommeroys
spend a great deal of time swimming, often (but not always) an activity
suggestive of purification in Cheever's fiction. But no matter what the
activity or occasion, Lawrence discovers something to disapprove of,
some way to make those around him miserable. Even Mrs. Pommeroy's cook Anna suffers under the glare of his uprightness. Tifty's in-
terference in her affairs takes the form of a patronizing concern that
succeeds only in alienating her, as she explains to the narrator: "He is
so skinny but he is always coming into my kitchen to pity me, but I
am as good as him, I am as good as *anybody*—" (11).

Like many of Cheever's fictional servants, Anna never rises above the level of caricature, yet her function here is important: she establishes the fact that like the communist Girsdansky of "In Passing," Lawrence is a stern idealist with no real constituency, a preacher without a following. If it is true that most of us are reasonably content with our lives most of the time, someone with as dour a view of life as Lawrence stands little chance of redeeming us.

The message of "Goodbye, My Brother" has further ramifications, however. Anna is content and even happy with her "menial" life (actually she loves to cook and is as obsessed with the need to feed people as Lawrence is driven to unsettle them), and on another level so is the narrator satisfied with his (he is happily married and teaches at a private secondary school). But the attention Cheever lavishes on the raw beauty of the New England seacoast and the vacationers at play on it offers a better insight into the story's ultimate meaning: "We drove back to Laud's Head. It had been a brilliant afternoon, but on the way home we could smell the east wind—the dark wind, as Lawrence would have said—coming in from the sea" (14–15). Above and beyond the preoccupations of everyday life, such passages suggest, there are moments or days when the heavens open to reveal the truth that life can be fine and beautiful, if only we allow it to be. Lawrence is not prepared to admit this, and that is why his brother, with some deliberation, almost kills him.

Like many short story writers, Cheever was a notetaker and journal keeper, and in a 1959 essay titled "What Happened" he describes the transformation, from notes to story, that occurred with "Goodbye, My Brother." In the process, he (perhaps unintentionally) sheds light on the problem of moral perspective in this story. In reviewing his notes, searching for a way to improve what was then a "bad" story, he writes:

> I came on the description of a friend who, having lost the charms of youth and unable to find any new lights to go by, had begun to dwell on his football triumphs. This was connected to a scathing description of the house in the Vineyard where we had spent a pleasant summer. The house had not been old, but it had been sheathed with old shingles and the new wood of the doors had been scored and stained. The rooms were lighted with electric candles and I linked this crude sense of the past to my friend's failure to mature. The failure, my notes said, was national. We had failed to mature as a people and had turned back to dwell on old football triumphs, raftered ceilings, candlelight and open fires. There were some tearful notes on the sea, washing away the embers of our picnic fires,

on the east wind—the dark wind—on the promiscuity of a beautiful
young woman I know. . . . The only cheerful notes in all this were
two sentences about the pleasure I had taken one afternoon in
watching my wife and another young lady walk out of the sea without any clothes on.[24]

Taking Cheever's "factual" statements literally is a risky thing at
best, but in this case he seems to be admitting that both Lawrence and
his brother had their genesis in a single narrative viewpoint—John
Cheever's. Two sides or "halves" of Cheever himself, in short, find
expression in "Goodbye, My Brother": the negative hypercritic and
the cheerful optimist. Understanding this might not make the story's
ethical ambiguity any less complicated, but it may clarify our sense of
both the narrative and its creator to realize that in having his narrator
wreak mayhem on Lawrence, Cheever is possibly trying to exorcise
one of his own demons.

The theme of life's essential goodness—the notion that although we
must continually struggle against evil wrought by others and ourselves,
there is reason to hope in a divine benevolence—would frequently
reappear in Cheever's fiction over the next twenty-five years, but with
diminishing resonance. Only after his emergence from the depths of
alcoholic despair would the same note be sounded with full conviction;
it reverberates powerfully in the conclusion of *Falconer*, Cheever's 1976
novel about a man who is sent to prison for murdering his brother.
"Goodbye, My Brother" never became part of a published novel (several Cheever stories are actually sections of the Wapshot novels, *Bullet
Park*, and *Falconer*), but it seems likely that the germ of the novel's
premise is to be found in this story, and perhaps in the troubled relationship between Cheever and his brother Fred.[25]

The storyteller in this case is only a would-be murderer, however.
As the evidence of Tifty's distaste for the joys of life mounts, Cheever
steadily works the reader's moral consciousness into a position
whereby, after an exchange of insults during a walk on the beach, as
the narrator picks up a piece of driftwood and hits Lawrence from behind, that consciousness may well acquiesce in the deed if not approve
it. As would-be "ethical" readers we may well *not* approve it, or his
stated wish to have his brother dead and "about to be buried, because
I did not want to be denied ceremony and decorum in putting him
away, in putting him out of my consciousness" (19), but as informed
"bystanders" we can hardly claim not to understand. Conversely, a

feeling of sympathy for the victim is astonishingly difficult to conjure up: has he not in effect provoked the narrator's rage by ruining everyone's vacation? And although that is undeniably the case, it is also true that the narrator has acted on impulse—"naturally," as it were.

And yet a crime has been committed. The fact that Lawrence survives, returns to the house, gathers his family and leaves with no intention of prosecuting his brother cannot override this point. Our acquiescence in that crime, purely fictional though it may be, implicates us in it. The final verdict in the case, however, centers not on the murderer manquè, but on the victim:

> Oh, what can you do with a man like that? What can you do? How can you dissuade his eye in a crowd from seeking out the cheek with acne, the infirm hand; how can you teach him to respond to the inestimable greatness of the race, the harsh surface beauty of life; how can you put his finger for him on the obdurate truths before which fear and horror are powerless? (21)

To confirm the rightness of his position, the narrator closes with a dreamlike picture of pagan naturalness that silently gives the lie to Tifty's unnatural Puritanism: "The sea that morning was iridescent and dark. My wife and my sister were swimming—Diana and Helen—and I saw their uncovered heads, black and gold in the water. I saw them come out and I saw that they were naked, unshy, beautiful, and full of grace, and I watched the naked women walk out of the sea" (21).

Another story from the early fifties, "O Youth and Beauty!" (1953),[26] celebrates spontaneity and the vigorous enjoyment of life and also ends on a strangely equivocal note. The title itself equivocates; it would appear to be a shout of praise, but in light of the death of the story's protagonist, Cash Bentley, an aging athlete who refuses to slow down as he grows older, it can be read as a cry of lament. The tale is set in Shady Hill, where Cash and his wife Louise and their two children live in "a medium-cost ranch house on Alewives Lane" (211). They are, in short, as "average" as the Westcotts of "The Enormous Radio," and as with the Westcotts, beneath the smooth exterior of their lives lurk serious problems. Money, or the lack of sufficient income to support the appearance of prosperity that the Bentleys want to promote for themselves, is their chief concern. Cash has not done well financially or professionally, and the couple's married life has been anything but smooth. Additionally, Cash has come to rely on whiskey as a simple solution to everyday problems.

Cheever's method of teasing out these hidden flaws in the Bentley family portrait is even more masterful than the one he devised for "The Enormous Radio," perhaps because there is no need to sustain a fantastic premise as the narrative moves relentlessly toward its violent conclusion. He sustains an effective balance between generalizations describing the suburban life-style and particular examples of both its felicity and its inexplicable sadness. The opening sentence, one of the longest Cheever ever wrote, paints a melancholy picture of a typical Saturday night party in Shady Hill, "when almost everybody who was going to play golf or tennis in the morning had gone home hours ago and the ten or twelve people remaining seemed powerless to bring the evening to an end" (210). It is here, in the vague hours between night and morning, that Cash and his friend Trace Bearden move furniture to fashion a series of hurdles that Cash will use in a vain attempt to recapture his youth. To start Cash on his run, Trace even fires a starter's pistol out a nearby window—a Chekhovian touch that foreshadows the story's end.

Generalization and particular example are skillfully combined, for example, when we learn that on more than one occasion, a "bad day at the office" has had serious repercussions for the Bentleys' relationship. These begin with shortness of temper on Cash's part and proceed to his drinking heavily and eventually to Louise's threatening to move in with her sister. But this is invariably prevented by the power of love (clichéd as it seems, the miraculous often takes the form of physical passion between husband and wife in Cheever's fiction), and the Bentleys revert to the affectionate behavior of newlyweds. The tidal rhythm of their marriage is shaken, however, when Cash breaks his leg trying to leap over a chest at a party given in honor of the Bentleys' seventeenth anniversary. The accident damages Cash's spirit more severely than his body, and his perception of the world around him starts to take on a depressingly macabre slant.

Cash's dark mood continues for several months, as spring advances into summer. One evening he observes the young people of his neighborhood enjoying themselves in that season of youth, but he can take no vicarious pleasure in their rituals: "Taxes and the elastic in underpants—all the unbeautiful facts of life that threaten to crush the breath out of Cash—have not touched a single figure in this garden. Then jealousy seizes him—such savage and bitter jealousy that he feels ill"

(216). This is devastating exposition, and it too is worthy of Chekhov at his best.

Well before his final fall, then, Cash has fallen from grace. To identify his moral shortcomings and leave it at that, however, seems pointless—and it may be significant that in 1953 Cheever was exactly the same age as his protagonist. When Cash regains enough strength to try the furniture hurdles again, and to make it to the end without serious injury (although he immediately collapses with fatigue), it is easy to sympathize with him. And with Louise, who comforts him in a brief scene strikingly reminiscent of Michelangelo's Pietà: "She knelt down beside him and took his head in her lap and stroked his thin hair" (217).

Louise's love for Cash is crucial to any interpretation of the story's final moments. On the following Sunday the Bentleys are invited out by friends, and once again Cash insists on running the hurdles. Trace Bearden being absent, Cash silently calls on Louise to fire the starter's pistol:

> when she went down, he was standing at the foot of the stairs holding the pistol out to her. She had never fired it before, and the directions he gave her were not much help.
>
> "Hurry up," he said, "I can't wait all night."
>
> He had forgotten to tell her about the safety, and when she pulled the trigger nothing happened.
>
> "It's that little lever," he said. "Press that little lever." Then, in his impatience, he hurdled the sofa anyhow.
>
> The pistol went off and Louise got him in midair. She shot him dead. (218)

Like the immortal youth on John Keats's Grecian urn, Cash Bentley never will grow old. Middle age brought him close enough to that detested goal, and we are left to wonder how accidental his death really was. There is no substantial reason for thinking that Louise hated him, although he undeniably made her life difficult. The parody of the Pietà, coming just before the story's conclusion as it does, suggests another reading: in the deepest recesses of their souls, both Cash and Louise understood full well that Cash was born to be an eternal twenty-one-year-old. Time had mercilessly outstripped that self-image, to the point that when Cash handed her the pistol, he was making a wordless compact with Death (emphatically not with Louise, although she is

Death's instrument), here seen as a deliverer. In effect Cash was already dead as he lay, quite literally spent, in Louise's comforting arms at the country club.

The following year a story called "Independence Day at St. Botolph's"[27] appeared in the 3 July edition of the *New Yorker*. Although its mood is even more nostalgic than the sad tale of Cash Bentley, its sense of regret at the disappearance of a wonderful past is tempered by a feeling of hopeful anticipation. The story centers on a Fourth of July celebration in a small New England town, and as a self-contained narrative it belongs to the "slice of New England life" genre; but anyone familiar with Cheever's novels would probably recognize it as an earlier version of the opening pages of *The Wapshot Chronicle*, winner of the National Book Award in 1957.

Following an introduction that establishes the homey, small-town atmosphere of St. Botolph's, the initial focus in the *New Yorker* version is on two boys, Moses and Coverly Wapshot, who "lived on a farm two miles below the village and had canoed upriver before dawn, when the night air made the water of the river feel tepid as it rose around the canoe paddle, over their hands. They had forced a window of Christ Church, as they always did, and had rung the bell, waking a thousand song birds" (18). Thus begins one of Cheever's more fruitful experiments with form and content; in this case, since the novel represents a finished product, the results are easier to see than in most others. A comparison of this early version with the opening section of the *Chronicle* offers some valuable insights into the workings of Cheever's imagination and demonstrates that although the original material was changed in several respects, the *Chronicle*'s central conflict and theme are presaged in the short story. In both cases, Cheever's main concerns were "the war between the sexes" and the consequent need of men who fare badly in that war to leave their homes on journeys of exploration. By considering the changes Cheever made in his original material, we can better understand the connections that exist between these related motifs. Moses and Coverly's canoe trip, it would appear, was merely the first twist in a long and fascinating narrative skein.

The short story is definitely set in the early 1930s, while the novel's Independence Day celebration is impossible to date precisely. Cheever explained this shift to what might be called deliberate vagueness in a letter to Frederick Bracher: "I have carefully avoided dates in order to give my characters freedom to pursue their emotional lives without the interruptions of history. . . . A sense of time that revolves around the sinking of ships and declarations of war seems to me a sense of time debased. We live at deeper levels than these and fiction should make this clear."[28] Cheever's narrative vision was notably wider when he wrote *The Wapshot Chronicle*. Moses and Coverly got slightly older, Moses progressing from sixteen to college age (probably twenty) and Coverly from twelve to sixteen or seventeen. It soon becomes evident in the novel that this added maturity is vital to Cheever's larger narrative aims; Moses and Coverly are about to become truly independent of St. Botolph's for the first time in their lives.

In the short story the Independence Day parade is held up—as in the novel—because the boys' mother has not yet taken her place of honor on the Woman's Club float. As the Club's founder and St. Botolph's leading civic improver, Sarah Wapshot is important enough to merit such consideration. But whereas this delay has no real significance in the *Chronicle*, in the story it serves to introduce the story's crux. When their mother finally appears, Moses and Coverly are struck by the fact that she has been crying. Following the celebration we learn why: her husband Alpheus (he becomes Leander in the novel) has stolen her jewelry, and she is certain that he has run off with a local widow to whom he has shown more than passing attention.

Mr. Wapshot's infidelity is central to his character here; the omniscient narrator reports that, frustrated by Sarah's social preoccupations, Alpheus has "consoled himself freely" with "boarding house widows, seaside girls, and other doxies" (19). This promiscuity is referred to at the beginning of the *Chronicle;* as the novel unfolds, however, its usefulness as an indicator of Leander's character fades. He undoubtedly would have been a less appealing protagonist in direct proportion to the anguish such behavior caused his wife.

In the original version, once the parade begins it proceeds without any difficulty, and thus does not receive any descriptive emphasis. Cheever has already depicted the town square by way of introduction: it is old, shaded, declining rather than vital. While all of this carries over into the *Chronicle* setting, there the day's festivities are interrupted when a firecracker goes off under the tail of the horse pulling Mrs. Wapshot's float. The subsequent wild ride and calmer return to the town permit the author to depict not just the exterior but also the soul of St. Botolph's as a base from which Moses and Coverly will soon launch their explorations. It is a town whose once manly spirit has fallen on hard times:

> At the junction of Hill and River streets the wagon turned right, passing George Humbolt's, who lived with his mother and who was known as Uncle Peepee Marshmallow. Uncle Peepee came from a line of hardy sailors but he was not as virile as his grandfathers. Could he, through yearning and imagination, weather himself as he would have been weathered by a passage through the straits of Magellan?[29]

Uncle Peepee's adventures in the less romantic present are confined to pathetic, naked rambles through the town's river gardens, and the local residents have come to accept him as almost a part of the scenery. As we have seen, the theme of the Northeast's declining vitality was of recurring interest to Cheever.

The *New Yorker* story has Mrs. Wapshot preparing a large family luncheon for the holiday. It is a logical, convenient way to assemble characters and gradually bring to a head the question raised by Alpheus's theft. Among the invited guests are Sarah's sister Hazel and brother-in-law Win, who do not figure in the novel (where the dinner serves more as a transition device), and Cousin Honora Wapshot, who decidedly does. Here she is described as an eccentric busybody who every Christmas Eve descends on Boston and infiltrates the carolers on Beacon Hill, "passing out antivivisectionist literature. This expressed her disapproval of Christmas" (22). She is also characterized as "belligerent" by the narrator, but he tempers this by conceding that her intentions are generally charitable. The chronicler or principal voice of the novel pictures her in essentially the same way; there, however, her eccentricity takes on greater thematic import. As the inheritor of a sizable fortune, amassed by earlier generations of seafaring Wapshots, she has a decisive voice in the affairs of Moses and Coverly. Her will stipulates that her money will be divided between them "contingent upon their having male heirs" (52). She also owns their home and their father's ferryboat, the *Topaze;* much later in the *Chronicle* Sarah will take control of the boat and convert it into a gift shop, thus precipitating the tragic decline of her husband.

The novel's sexual antagonism is definitely prefigured in the story's postluncheon scene. Sarah convinces Hazel and Win that Alpheus has forsaken her, and to be helpful Win suggests that he might be able to find work for Moses. In despair, Sarah admits that her husband has somehow managed to gain and keep the affection of their sons:

" 'Moses loves him,' Mrs. Wapshot sobbed. 'I'm afraid that Moses may try to follow him. Moses tries to imitate him. And yet he loved his hound dog more than he loved Moses'" (23). As for Coverly, Sarah laments that she "tried so hard to protect him," adding that she didn't want either of her sons to be born. The reader supplies the aspersion: "to a father like Alpheus."

The irony of the boys' love for their father pervades the *Chronicle* and may, in fact, help to explain much of its action. As a motive force, it cuts in more than one direction. For if Moses and Coverly reject their mother's overprotectiveness in favor of their father's joie de vivre, they must also achieve more than their father has been able to. Leander is homebound, tied down to St. Botolph's, his wife, and Cousin Honora. His boat, the *Topaze,* is actually a melancholy reminder of the Wapshots' storied past. Named for sailing ships on which earlier generations of Wapshot men voyaged to places like Samoa and Ceylon, Leander's vessel is a decaying, ramshackle convenience for tourists. Over the years Leander has adjusted to his dependent situation; he even revels in his standing as a local character—a more reputable version of Uncle Peepee. But in his lack of independence lies a terrible vulnerability, a danger against which his sons are not quite so defenseless because they are free to explore.

The short story's conclusion hints strongly at this. It is a superficially heartwarming, but typically ironic, Cheeverian closing. Honora, who has been on the trail of a mockingbird in a neighbor's pasture, is now seen running across his field chased by a cow. At the last second Win pulls her to safety, just as Alpheus is sighted blithely piloting the *Topaze* up the river to the Wapshot homestead: "He had stolen the jewelry, and spent the fifty dollars he got for it on fireworks. He was in high spirits, for he knew there would never again be such a display on the farm" (23).

The story's final image, however, centers on Moses and Coverly sitting on the lawn, the older boy's arm draped over his brother's shoulder. Taking up a self-comforting remark by his mother, in which she contrasts her suffering with that of "the people of Armenia," Moses expresses a vision that directly foreshadows the *Chronicle*'s chief preoccupation:

> Moses threw his arm around Coverly's shoulder. "You know, we'll go all over the place," he said, sitting on the grass. The mention of Armenia and a charge of animal spirits accounted for the remark, but

he meant much more than the bare facts of travel. He meant a reasonable freedom to move among ideas and places and faces. "We'll
go all over the place," he said, "you and I." He was so right. (23)

Through Honora's direct intervention, in the *Chronicle* Moses and
Coverly will be forced out of St. Botolph's and compelled to test themselves against the rigors of the outside world. Initially each will make
a poor showing: Moses as a foreign service trainee who gets himself
entangled in a foolish liaison with a married woman; Coverly as a
would-be businessman in New York. Even when each finds the "right"
woman for him, the Wapshot penchant for difficult relationships resur-
faces and stalks the brothers down the pathways of their marriages.
Haunted by the specter of an abusive stepfather,[30] Coverly's wife,
Betsey, pushes him to the brink of homosexuality. Moses finds himself
competing against his Aunt Justina for the affection of her lovely but
overprotected ward, the orphaned Melissa Scaddon. He wins, but at
great emotional cost to both himself and his wife. Still, compared to
their father, both sons have achieved a measure of freedom by the end
of the *Chronicle*—and before he dies that is Leander's greatest comfort.

Thus "Independence Day at St. Botolph's" was a rich seedbed for
the narrative detail and themes of *The Wapshot Chronicle*. In particular,
the short story presages the sexual conflicts and journeys of discovery
that are unifying elements of the *Chronicle*. In this case the short story
form was clearly not sufficient to Cheever's purposes: Moses's unde-
fined dream is a vague but somehow exhilarating promise that looks
forward to the "ideas and places and faces" of the *Chronicle*. Moses,
Coverly—indeed, all of the Wapshots—had far to go.

Eden Reconsidered

Cheever returned to Shady Hill in 1954 with a crash. "The Country Husband," another Cheever "classic," begins with a plane crash-landing in a cornfield near Philadelphia.[31] Francis Weed, the story's anti-hero, survives along with the rest of the passengers and crew, but we soon discover that his survival has merely opened the door to a series of misfortunes, most of them marital. The melancholy business of both "The Season of Divorce" and "O Youth and Beauty!" is carried forward, and the depth of Cheever's night vision more fully exploited, in this story. In its Lawrence Pommeroy–like insistence on uncovering the serpent hiding beneath the flowers of suburban domesticity, it is representative of most of Cheever's fiction of the later fifties and beyond.

The first person Weed attempts to confide in concerning his brush with death is Trace Bearden, Cash Bentley's friend. Weed meets Bearden on the train to Shady Hill and, in a foreshadowing of what awaits him at home, is impolitely ignored. When he finally gets home and starts to explain what has happened, pandemonium breaks out among his children, and the story of the most harrowing experience of his life never gets told. Like the precariously married couple in "The Season of Divorce"—like so many of Cheever's couples and so many in real life—the Weeds have allowed time and their children to drive a wedge between them. That alteration and a broader sense of discontent with his life combine to make Francis vulnerable to the charms of an innocent babysitter, Anne Murchison. While taking her home after her first evening with his children, Francis sees that she is distraught. He draws from her the revelation that her father is an alcoholic and that he has accused her of immoral behavior. Weed's sympathy slides easily into a comforting (but chaste) embrace, and thence into love.

Shady Hill may not be Salem, but the dilemma posed by this moral declension is as difficult a problem for Francis Weed as that faced by Nathaniel Hawthorne's Mr. Dimmesdale. Although Anne never tries to seduce him, she (again, quite innocently) tends to encourage rather than discourage his interest. Bravely, he squares off against sin and insomnia by trying to concentrate on more acceptable diversions, searching for something "that would injure no one, and he thought of skiing. Up through the dimness in his mind rose the image of a mountain deep in snow. It was late in the day. Wherever his eyes looked, he saw broad and heartening things." Then the waking dream fades, and the following day he arrives at an initial but clearly unsatisfactory resolution of his ethical problem; he simply refuses to see it as a problem. "It was a clear morning; the morning seemed to put him into a relationship to the world that was mysterious and enthralling. Cars were beginning to fill up the [train station] parking lot, and he noticed that those that had driven down from the high land above Shady Hill were white with hoarfrost. This first clear sign of autumn thrilled him" (333). But this cheery sense of exhilaration is a false note. In a startling transformation, it deteriorates into snappishness in a short and apparently comic conversation with the elderly Mrs. Wrightson, whom Cheever does not identify until later in the story. As they wait for the next train to the city, Mrs. Wrightson launches into a long, boring soliloquy on a set of window curtains she has purchased, concluding, "and you can imagine what a problem they present. I don't know what to do with them." Cheever the writer of television situation comedy has given Francis Weed the rejuvenated lover a perfect straight line, and he responds accordingly: "'I know what you can do with them,' Francis said. 'What?' 'Paint them black on the inside, and shut up.'" (334).

This lightens the somber mood of the story, but it also has serious repercussions—aftershocks that point to Cheever's growing interest in exploring moral implications rather than implying that situations like Francis Weed's can be easily worked out. At this point in its fictional history, the very air of Shady Hill is still redolent of Christian uprightness (although the longer we follow Cheever down its winding paths, the more we come to suspect the nature of that aroma): "Looking back over the recent history of Shady Hill for some precedent, he found there was none. There was no turpitude; there had not even been a breath of scandal. Things seemed arranged with more propriety even than in the Kingdom of Heaven" (335). The story's most poignant moment is one fraught with irony: a photographer arrives to take the Weeds' Christmas card picture; before Francis joins Julia and the children, he writes Anne a maudlin love letter, and when "Julia called him to come down, the abyss between his fantasy and the practical world opened so wide that he felt it affected the muscles of his heart" (337).

Irony hardens into absurdity when Francis discovers that Anne is engaged to a young man who shares his disillusionment with Shady Hill, and whose very callowness makes him a much more appropriate lover for the girl. Immediately following this crushing revelation, Julia tells him that as a result of his behavior on the train platform they have been conspicuously not invited to a party by Mrs. Wrightson, whom we now learn "runs Shady Hill and has run it for forty years" (340). More particularly she has the power to advance, or ruin, the social chances of the Weeds' eldest daughter, Helen. Julia's indictment of Francis's thoughtlessness is devastating and cogent, but it reduces him to wordless depravity. He hits her in the face—perhaps the only time this occurs in Cheever's work—and thus sets the scene for another sad, but far from tragic denouement.

The ensuing dialogue between husband and wife represents Cheever at the height of his technical powers in the handling of such exchanges. It is essentially a reconciliation scene, although Francis has yet to arrive at the moral crossroads where he will be forced to choose between good and evil. Francis is simply and pathetically sorry for his maltreatment of Julia, and he insists that he loves her. She responds with some amateur psychologizing that turns into a richly comic moment:

> "You have no idea of how much you hate me. I think it's subconscious. You don't realize the cruel things you've done."
> "What cruel things, Julia?"
> "The cruel acts your subconscious drives you to in order to express your hatred of me."
> "What, Julia?"
> "I've never complained."
> "Tell me."
> "Your clothes."
> "What do you mean?"
> "I mean the way you leave your dirty clothes around in order to express your subconscious hatred of me." (341)

The exchange functions as light comic dialogue on its face, but given the events leading up to it—Francis's flirtation with Anne Murchison and, by extension, marital disaster—it also succeeds on another, more significant level. As a crystallizing moment in the story, it forces us to consider the pathetic condition of a husband whose intended infidelity could be discovered at any moment, even as we are reassured, in effect, that things will probably turn out all right for him and his family.

But what is the meaning of "all right" in this story? In a scene reminiscent of "O Youth and Beauty!" Julia eventually succumbs to Francis's pleas that she remain. Given this second chance, Francis considers his options, which range from getting drunk (although he includes raping Anne as a "choice," this seems intended for effect and not to be taken seriously) to seeing a psychiatrist. Interestingly, although religion was mentioned in passing in "O Youth and Beauty!" as a mere set of forms without meaning in Cash Bentley's life, it is not even referred to here. Francis chooses a psychiatrist, whose recommended therapy is woodworking, a course of treatment that appears to satisfy the patient. In the end the narrator informs us simply that "Francis is happy" as we look over his shoulder in the basement of his home, nestled snugly in the secure environment of a Shady Hill that has once again settled into countless routines of reassuring domesticity.

Yet the restoration of order in the life of Francis Weed and his family appears to come at a very high price. Unlike Cash Bentley, he is condemned to life: rather than being allowed to escape the constraints imposed by the social framework called Shady Hill, he is forced to admit that for him there is really only one choice—"happiness" in the form of a conventional existence. He was not born to seduce beautiful young women and run off to the South Seas with them, or to degenerate into alcoholic dementia on Skid Row—another kind of romantic excess. He was born, in the words of Samuel Beckett, to go on.

For a stern Puritan temperament, this is hardly satisfactory. Francis has sinned; should he not be punished severely? The story's last sentence, which follows a comforting description of some neighborhood pets and their antics, hints (and once more Cheever prefers ambiguity to moral-pointing) that Francis's happiness is of the sort enjoyed by model prisoners: "Then it is dark; it is a night where kings in golden suits ride elephants over the mountains" (346). The line is often cited as proof of Cheever's characteristic tendency to soar fancifully, now and again, over the mundane topography of his suburban landscape. It is a logical choice to make the point, but it can also be seen in other lights. Like a good chess player, and countless literary practitioners before him, Cheever was capable of using a single device for multiple purposes simultaneously. The romantic image here is effective as a conclusion because it is so startling—but why so? It clearly harkens back to heroic deeds in faraway lands, and thus "puts Shady Hill in its place"; in this sense it has a mildly comic ring. An entire generation of Americans had invested a good deal of emotional as well as "real" capital in the creation of such Edens; Cheever seems to mock their expense of spirit as a "waste of shame," in Shakespeare's phrase. But as John Irving has noted,[32] when Cheever adopts a critical stance, one can usually detect a sympathetic undertone in his voice. He dwelt in a version of Shady Hill himself, and in fashioning a beautiful, highly rhetorical flourish to close the story of Francis Weed, he could be asking us not to condemn his nonhero. If Francis has chosen to reject sin out of his preoccupation with what the neighbors might think, then in the words of T. S. Eliot, he has done the right thing for the wrong reason—and thus committed the greatest treason. But if, as the reconciliation scene between Francis and Julia would have it, he genuinely loves his wife and has simply decided not to destroy the security of his family, who among us would step forward to cast the first stone at him?

Francis Weed stopped just short of a serious misstep. Johnny Hake, "The Housebreaker of Shady Hill" (1956),[33] definitely oversteps the bounds of legality by becoming a thief. His crime is all the more serious because Johnny is an accepted, respectable member of Shady Hill's polite society; in violating the property of his friends, he subverts the assumptions on which life in suburban America rests. The fact that he ultimately returns to the same kind of respectability that enfolds Francis Weed and most of Cheever's suburbanites—the inescapable fact that Cheever stage-manages a conclusion in which Johnny, having escaped detection as a burglar, happily anticipates the rosiest of futures—strains credulity and lends credence to critics like John Aldridge who fault Cheever for his "easy" resolutions to difficult problems.

Johnny Hake's portrait is drawn in many of the same hues as those of Cash Bentley and Francis Weed. At thirty-six he can look back at the first half of his life with smug satisfaction in its WASPish "rightness": "raised on Sutton Place, christened and confirmed in St. Bartholomew's, . . . I . . . met my wife (Christina Lewis) at one of those big cotillions at the Waldorf" (253). The Hakes have four children and, in this best of all possible worlds, enough innate goodness to see them through. As Johnny opens his own story, he paints a picture of a genuinely happy family life, guided by himself as a husband and father who—unlike many of his Shady Hill neighbors—values his happiness rightly.

Trouble in this instance comes from without rather than within. It takes the form of Johnny's being unjustly fired from a lucrative job in New York. Cheever sets the moral background for the story when Johnny reveals that prior to being let go he had been ordered by the company's owner to fire the man who subsequently sacks him. Out of softhearted sympathy for the man and his family, Johnny had delayed letting him go, allowing him time to rebound from alcoholism. Far from being the best of possible worlds, then, Johnny's piece of the pie is a bitter slice of the American business environment in the twentieth century.

The problem Johnny faces is thus all too familiar, and unbearably real in human terms. He can take the mechanical steps involved in starting a job search easily enough, but how to explain to Christina and their children what has happened? In a flood of protective sentiment, he decides not to: "There seemed to be as much truth in her beauty and the power she exerted over my senses as there was in the fact that we were overdrawn at the bank" (253).

But love will not suffice to cover the overdrafts, Johnny knows. And he cannot look to his widowed mother, who hates Christina, for help. After a particularly unpleasant dinner party and an unnerving premonition of death brought on by a coughing fit, Johnny decides in the middle of the night to rob the Warburtons, his dinner hosts. The deed itself, in the era preceding home protection alarms, proves almost childishly simple to execute; he walks into their home and steals a wallet containing almost a thousand dollars.

The realization of what he has done at first breeds panic, then shame and guilt. This reaction is only exacerbated by his vivid sense of Shady Hill's prettiness and moral rectitude: "Urged to build bomb shelters, they plant trees and roses, and their gardens are splendid and bright. Had I looked, the next morning, from my bathroom window into the evil-smelling ruin of some great city, the shock of recalling what I had done might not have been so violent, but the moral bottom had dropped out of my world without changing a mote of sunlight" (258). The contrast between the fair order of Shady Hill and the foul disorder of his spirit is strong enough to override any incipient self-justification. Johnny understands what he has done and calls himself a "child of darkness" without a trace of irony.

To this point Cheever has constructed a marvel of a story, worthy of a modern Hawthorne. But when Johnny returns to his cubicle in the city to resume his job hunting, the appropriately dark shading of the narrative lightens to an almost absurd gray before brightening incredibly into dawnlike splendor. The transformation happens so subtly—with the artist in full control of his brushes even as his powers of conception are faltering—as to be almost unnoticeable. But it wrecks the story.

As he reads the newspaper, Johnny searches out incidents of theft and burglary rather than job openings, and those he finds bring solace when he compares them with his own relatively minor offense. He sees a customer in a restaurant pocket a tip left by someone else and catches himself thinking "What a crook!" When a friend presses him to enter a shady business deal with the joking line, "Now, in order to participate in this burglary, all you have to do . . . " (263), Johnny becomes physically ill—and we smile at the psychological accuracy of Cheever's brushwork. Yet something is amiss between the lines, in the cracks that form between style and substance; Cheever has sensed the comic possibilities of his material and has chosen to play that material for laughs rather than explore it for ideas. Recalling his avoidance of this trap in stories like "The Enormous Radio" and "The Country Husband," a thoughtful reader might accept John Aldridge's criticism (directed primarily at the novels) that Cheever's "most aberrant effects are not only represented in the clichés of aberration . . . but are often neutralized by some last-minute withdrawal from the full implication of their meaning, some abrupt whimsical detour into palliating fantasy. . . . All discordant extremes of conduct and perception are finally absorbed into a fundamentally equable view of life."[34] In "The Housebreaker of Shady Hill" the detour takes us down the path of comedy rather than fantasy. Some of the comic touches are masterful and inspired—as, for example, Johnny's moment of near-breakdown when his children surprise him with the gift of an extension ladder for his birthday—but regardless of the detour's direction, the effect is the same: we desperately want to get back on the main narrative road because the inconsistency in tone is too glaring. Simply put, Cheever's endless search for light occasionally led him astray, and "The Housebreaker of Shady Hill" is one example.

This inconsistency is also evident in Johnny's painstaking attempt to psychoanalyze himself—an effort that recapitulates his almost nonexistent relationship with his father and ends with a ludicrous rationalization that vitiates his earlier self-criticism: "It had not been my fault that I had stolen then [in his youth, from his father], and it had not been my fault when I went to the Warburtons'. It was my father's fault!" (261). Johnny's subsequent recollection that his father has been dead for fifteen years deflates whatever serious or comic value this section of the story may have had or pretended to.

Although the Hakes come closer to a marital split than the Bentleys, in the end they are saved by a deus ex machina, when Johnny's former boss dies suddenly and he is recalled to his former job. In the meantime Johnny has had a change of heart (brought on by nothing more than the patter of rain on his head) about stealing, and at the story's close he breaks into the Warburtons' to return the exact amount he had stolen. This is not fantasy but it is a close cousin, and forced in a sense that Cheever did not intend. As Eugene Chesnick has pointed out, some readers will feel cheated, and wonder how Cheever would have handled what is certainly promising story material without such contrivances.[35] What if Johnny had burgled several homes successfully, and then got caught? The situation would have been less humorous; but Cheever's gifts, pushed in such a direction, would almost certainly have made it more enlightening.

In the following year, 1957, Cheever showed once again that he was capable of confronting difficult issues head on rather than having to construct byways around them. Once again he chose marital strife as his subject matter, and as in "The Season of Divorce," the vulnerability of a wife to an attentive male other than her husband is his theme. "The Trouble of Marcie Flint"[36] is a story rarely given serious critical attention, perhaps because its plot and structure seem so idiosyncratic. But it is a prime example of Cheever at his experimental best, and I would suggest that it offers convincing proof that Cheever could write about female emotions in a sympathetic, nonpatronizing manner. Three years earlier, in a story called "The Five-Forty-Eight," Cheever had shown sympathetic interest in the plight of women employees victimized by predatory bosses; although the story in its telling is nonjudgmental, the fact that the victim is finally able to confront and punish her boss on her own terms seems to speak for itself. In "The Trouble of Marcie Flint" the wronged party is Marcie's husband, Charlie Flint, a businessman and denizen of Shady Hill. The story's crux is a brief affair between Marcie and Noel Mackham, with whom she has joined forces to argue for a public library (Cheever has a good deal of fun caricaturing the opponents of the library, and of learning in general, in Shady Hill).

The experimental nature of the story—and we should recall that by this time Cheever had been publishing stories for twenty-seven years—can be seen in its opening paragraphs. At first the narrator appears to be Charlie Flint himself, who begins with a diatribe (in a journal entry written aboard a ship headed for Italy) against the domestic emptiness of suburban living: "What holes! The suburbs, I mean. God preserve me from the lovely ladies taking in their asters and their roses at dusk lest the frost kill them, and from ladies with their heads whirling with civic zeal. I'm off to Torino, where the girls love peanut butter and the world is a man's castle and . . . " (289). What Charlie has barely hinted at, and what Cheever prefers to develop slowly rather than reveal early, is that Charlie has left Marcie soon after discovering one of the unintended consequences of such civic zeal.

Our lack of awareness on this point aside, it would be quite easy for us as readers to take this opening salvo as representing Cheever's "position" on the events that follow; here is the master storyteller-critic lashing out, once and for all, at the terminal niceness of pseudopastoral America. But Charlie's remarks are immediately followed by another narrator's gloss, a commentary that carefully distances the story's frame from Charlie's version of things: "There was absolutely nothing wrong with the suburb (Shady Hill) from which Charles Flint was fleeing, his age is immaterial, and he was no stranger to Torino" (289). Did Cheever himself hate suburbia? In story after story, the answer, in Sam Goldwyn's phrase, is a definite "maybe."

The story line alternates between Charlie's shipboard record of prior events—necessarily limited by his absence from most of them—and the observations of an omniscient third-person narrator; this "split focus" has important implications for a fuller interpretation of the story. The narrator tells us that like "all bitter men, Flint knew less than half the story and was more interested in unloading his own peppery feelings than in learning the truth" (288). Part of that truth is that Charlie's prolonged absences from home on business led Marcie to accept a seat on the Village Council, the first in a series of steps leading inevitably to her infatuation with the equally civic-minded Noel Mackham. And this too is an essential feature of the narrative: none of the main characters trapped in its center is guilty of any bad or stupid intentions; none is even unlikable. On the contrary, their intentions are uniformly good or noble, and their personalities pleasant. Whereas Dr. Trencher of "The Season of Divorce" could be taken as a fool or a scoundrel or both, Mackham has all the disarming public spirit and quiet strength of a Jimmy Stewart film character. The fact that he comes from "the wrong side of the tracks"—he lives in Maple Dell, "the kind of place where the houses stand cheek by jowl, all of them white frame, all of them built twenty years ago" (291), seems only to add to his stature. Another unpleasant truth, however, is that somehow he and Marcie fall in love and that both are mature enough to understand what is happening to them.

Charlie Flint has no inkling of these developments until it is too late, and the manner of his finding out is dramatic enough to constitute a story in itself. One afternoon the Flints' young son and daughter mistake ant poison that Charlie has absentmindedly left in the refrigerator for candy, and eat it. The resulting crisis is frightening enough to mislead readers into anticipating a tragic outcome, but thematically its chief significance lies in its effect on Marcie, who was asleep when the accidental poisoning occurred. After the children have been ministered to by a doctor and their return to good health is assured, she announces to Charlie that she wants a divorce. She tells him that she sees the accident as "retribution" for the "mess" she has become entangled in with Noel Mackham.

Surprisingly, Cheever then briefly falls back on stock situation comedy by reversing the Flints' emotional states. In stunned silence, Charlie submits to a verbal outburst as Marcie's guilt turns inexplicably into accusation: "'Oh, I knew you'd be like this, I knew you'd be like this, I knew you'd blame me,' she said" (299). And on, and on. But then Cheever reins in the impulse to comic disintegration. It is a saddened Charlie who walks (or sails) away and a wiser Charlie who will eventually return to his children, his home, his wife. Before we learn of that final intention, the unnamed third-person narrator lets us observe the events leading up to Marcie's undoing, and this added insight establishes her lack of conscious illicit desire beyond any doubt. (Cheever draws the veil of ambiguity over her unconscious emotions, and Mackham's, however.) In this penultimate scene, Cheever underscores the folly of snap moral judgments by having a latter-day Puritan, Councilman Mark Barrett, deliver a stern warning to Marcie about the danger of encouraging Mackham's attention. Barrett's vulgar bluntness and lack of humanity so offend Marcie that his warning has the opposite effect: it virtually assures Mackham of more than a sympathetic hearing when he arrives to discuss the library project.

"The Trouble of Marcie Flint" thus shows us Cheever interweaving narrative voices with skill sufficient to produce an harmonic effect from their discordant tones, deftly juggling serious and comic effects, and most interesting of all, extending the range of his sympathies to include an unfaithful wife. Charlie concludes: "I will see my children grow and take up their lives, and I will gentle Marcie—sweet Marcie, dear Marcie, Marcie my love. I will shelter her with the curve of my body from all the harms of the dark" (301). The almost biblical, incantatory ring of this pledge leaves little doubt that Cheever wants us to take it seriously, and its position determines the centrality of its message. Unbending sternness and retribution may be the dictates of a Puritan emphasis on Old Testament values, but the new dispensation gives equal emphasis to love and forgiveness.

Over the fifty-year span of his career, Cheever often returned to techniques and themes that had served his narrative purposes well. In "The Lowboy" (1959)[37] he once again invokes the spellbinding power of symbolism demonstrated in "The Enormous Radio" and combines it with the flair for macabre fantasy first seen in "The Torch Song" to create a moral allegory grounded in the same kind of unbrotherly antagonism that drives such narratives as "Goodbye, My Brother" and *Falconer*. Cheever's unique brand of alchemy was capable of yielding disappointing results, as we have seen. In this case the reworking of tested elements is more successful in that "The Lowboy" is a compact, controlled story, of a kind rare in Cheever's published canon for its thematic bluntness. That bluntness, however, has its drawbacks.

The first-person narrator (as in "Goodbye, My Brother") is a character in his story, and he makes his hatred of his brother clear at once. If that puts the reader on guard and demands justification, the narrator is ready to explain it. His brother Richard is not only "small" physically—a poor reason—he is "spoiled" and thus small emotionally. This claim is supported by the events of the story, centered on Richard's acquisition of a valuable heirloom, a lowboy that has been in the family for generations. As it happens, an aging cousin has held such items in her possession until the last possible moment, and the narrator responds to the announcement that she is ready to part with them by asking for the lowboy. Richard's selfishness is evident in his insistence that he should have it, just as the storyteller's reliability is verified in his peeved willingness to part with it. Pressed to explain himself, Richard at first seems puzzled, then explains that the lowboy represents for him "the center of our life before Mother died" (405) and the happiness he associates with that life. Recalling the nastiness of the story's beginning, we may suspect the accuracy of Richard's memory; that suspicion is eventually borne out in a burst of spectral imaginings by the "good" brother.

In the interim, however, the lowboy must be moved from the narrator's home to Richard's, in the back of a station wagon whose carrying space is too small for the purpose. Once again Cheever the comedian can be detected behind the scenes, rigging his plot for comic effect; when the station wagon is hit from behind at a tollbooth and Richard explodes at the hapless tailgater, the scene is certainly funny, but entirely predictable. To be fair, it is also more consistent with the cynical tone of the story as a whole, and with the dramatic center of the piece. This is a procession of family ghosts conjured up by the narrator, a device conceived with the same imaginative power that Cheever displays in "The Enormous Radio" and "The Swimmer." Unfortunately, the sexual politics of this section reveal a misogyny so intense as to cast the merits of stories like "The Trouble of Marcie Flint" into real doubt.

The storyteller pictures Richard at home, alone, "drinking whiskey and admiring his creation" (409). He has arranged for a cabinetmaker to repair the lowboy and has duplicated its original setting as closely as possible. It is appropriate, then, for Cheever to distance himself from the black magic of the story by having Richard remember the dead aunts and uncles who have left their fingerprints on the lowboy's surface: appropriate but not quite honest. The narrator insists that it is Richard who, by recalling these dead souls, "evokes" them"—as if they had been waiting in pain and impatience all those years for his invitation" (409). But it is the narrator and the Prospero who gave him life who wish to imagine Richard suffering. It is the moralist in each of them that wants to see his grasping selfishness backfire.

The parade begins with Grandmother Delancey, "all dressed in black and smelling of ginger" (409). She is a physically impressive woman who made her presence felt in the vanguard of feminist politics earlier in the century, and "left her mark" in another significant manner—through her children. Unhappily their lives represent a catalog of failure and folly, and the narrator's point seems to be that their maternal source has something to do with that. Aunt Louisa is even more flamboyant than her mother, a failed painter who pressures her son into a musical career and suicide at the age of fifteen. Her husband, Uncle Tom, is a relentless womanizer who pushes Louisa down a flight of stairs, crippling a second, unborn child for life. Aunt Mildred inherits

Grandmother Delancey's passion for female emancipation, takes a lover, and turns her husband, Sidney, into an alcoholic. In the narrator's dream of their gathering, Sidney drops a lighted cigarette onto a sofa, starting a fire that ends the reverie in a blur of demented chaos. But in the "reality" of the story, a later visit to Richard's home reveals him to be as unhappy and mean-spirited as one would expect the victim of such an episode to be. The moral paradigm to be drawn from this is put in the form of a question that repeats the thematic enigma of "Goodbye, My Brother": "Oh, why is it that life is for some an exquisite privilege and others must pay for their seats at the play with a ransom of cholers, infections, and nightmares?" (411).

Without pausing to consider the Calvinist implications of the question, the storyteller carries the point so far as to destroy all of the family treasures in his possession. In his rage against material objects he becomes something of a preacher himself: "Hock the ruby necklace, throw away the invitation to Buckingham Palace, jump up and down on the perfume atomizer from Murano and the Canton fish plates. Dismiss whatever molests us and challenges our purpose, sleeping or waking. Cleanliness and valor will be our watchwords. Nothing less will get us past the armed sentry and over the mountainous border" (412). Nothing less will get us beyond our absorption in the mundane trivia of our lives, Richard's brother insists, half-seriously and half-mockingly; nothing less than a willingness to turn against the banal materialism of a culture that has retained the grasping worldliness of the Puritans and forsaken their spirituality. Further, if the Puritan in us insists on finding the origins of present evil in the wrongs of past generations, why not destroy at least the visible remnants of our ancestors' sinful existence?

Everything that Cheever has ever said or written for public consumption on the subject of personal values, whether in his fiction or as a statement of personal belief (his penchant for stretching the truth notwithstanding) gives this rejection of materialism the ring of authority. Although a persona or invented narrator delivers the statement, once again its position at the end of the story suggests it is a commentary on the shallowness of trust in material objects as a source of security and pleasure. But if this is true, we must also recognize that as a moral stand it represents one half of a paradox. As Samuel Coale has suggested, in cataloging his brother's sins the narrator is really exorcising his own inner darkness.[38] It is the narrator, after all, who conjures the ghost-gallery; who even on a beautiful spring day feels "it was the shadow that was most mysterious and exciting, the light one could not define" (405). In this "light," then, "The Lowboy" is a more sedate variation on the ethical and psychological themes explored earlier in "Goodbye, My Brother." In neither story, however, does the storyteller seem ready to turn the mirror held up to his brother's face on himself. Both tellers, in tales filled with ethical judgments, suffer from moral myopia. And it is this contradiction that lies at the heart of much of the critical and scholarly disagreement about the lasting value of Cheever's work.

For if Cheever was sincerely and consistently a seeker after the light and truth that occasionally break through the darkness of the human condition, one can also detect in his work—and, unfortunately in his life—a readiness to lose himself in that darkness. We see this tendency in his fairly consistent view of suburban life and materialism as just one more manifestation of human diversity—sometimes funny, sometimes sad, but fundamentally quite all right.[39] And we see it in his increasing preoccupation, in the stories of the fifties and sixties, with the outward signs of inward decay: alcoholism, marital strife, and criminal behavior. Certainly the first two of these plagued his personal life. It is as if, in many of his tales, there is a thematic subtext that is never fully expressed, even though the material of the story is plain enough. Johnny Hake may survive his flirtation with crime and even go on to a happy future, and the Flints will presumably patch up their marriage and continue to love each other. That is hopeful and encouraging on a purely human level, and short stories that attempt to scale the heights of tragedy seldom succeed, as Cheever well knew. Taken all in all, however, Cheever's stories from this period can be seen or heard as a desperate complaint: behind the lovely or stylish exteriors of modern American homes and offices, things are not going well at all; in fact, they are often going quite badly.

The Dream Unravels

By the late fifties Cheever had developed a unique narrative style that combined the hard-edged realism of his early work with lyrical accents capable of expressing poetic sentiment. Almost thirty years of experience had sharpened his artistic judgment to the point where his selection of realistic or fanciful effects was now almost unerring. He could "count the olives in a dish as quick as John O'Hara,"[40] in his words, or sing the loveliness of an autumn sunset over Shady Hill—and the terrible loneliness that accompanied it.

Recognition of his accomplishments started to arrive at the Cheevers' home in Scarborough in the form of awards and accolades. He won an O. Henry Award in 1956 for "The Country Husband" and was elected to the prestigious National Institute of Arts and Letters the following year. In 1958 the success of his first novel, *The Wapshot Chronicle*, earned him a National Book Award. The long years spent learning and mastering his craft now seemed to be bearing the sweet fruit of success. But something was wrong. The increased acceptance by his peers failed to bring him a sense of personal satisfaction. If anything, he became more despairing.

At a 1960 writers' conference in San Francisco, Cheever expressed his disgust with contemporary American life more directly (and melodramatically) than he had dared to in his fiction: "having determined the nightmare symbols of our existence, the characters have become debased and life in the United States in 1960 is hell," he insisted. He called attention to the "abrasive and faulty surface of the United States in the last twenty-five years" and concluded that the "only possible position for a writer now is negation."[41]

Even after allowing for rhetorical overstatement, this suggests that Cheever's social conscience, nonspecific though it may be in most of his stories, was still as sensitive as it had been in the 1930s. An avowedly nonpolitical writer, he may have had second thoughts about his generally consistent avoidance of "hot" or topical issues. But the anger in his remarks seems to transcend social concerns; hell, after all, is what the individual sinner makes it. Ostensibly Cheever had done everything that could reasonably be expected of a serious literary artist. He had refused to rest content with meeting other people's expectations for him and had branched out in new directions. Yet as the rewards for his diligence began to arrive, it almost seemed as if he had reached this stage of his career only to discover, in Gertrude Stein's phrase, that in terms of personal contentment there was no "there" there. Over the next several years, the tone of his stories would become increasingly introspective and bitter. Although he and the persona of his narrator are never precisely identical, these stories sound like the work of a man fighting a losing battle with psychological fatigue. More often than not, his lyrical voice shades perceptibly into tones of lamentation.

The strain between Cheever's personal desire to be an optimist and the demands of his craft is nowhere more evident than in a series of sketches that has appeared in two different versions, originally as "Some People, Places, and Things That Will Not Appear in My Next Novel" in the *New Yorker* (12 November 1960) and subsequently in an anthology with the same title, minus a section that parodies fellow writer J. D. Salinger. (The shorter version appears in *The Stories of John Cheever*, inaccurately titled "A Miscellany of Characters That Will Not Appear."[42] Not all of the sketches are concerned with characters.) This series of sketches is often cited in studies of Cheever's work, on the assumption that since the storyteller is clearly a writer rather than a conventional narrative observer or participant in a story, he represents Cheever himself. But Cheever's insistence on separating his life from his stories is at least as germane in this instance as it is in analyses of his more conventional fiction. This separation is crucial, furthermore, to a clear understanding of the unresolved tension between dogged cheerfulness and oppressive despair in much of his mature work. The equating of Cheever and the "voice" of these sketches is logical enough on the surface, but is fundamentally inaccurate.

The first exclusion in the "Miscellany" is a pretty girl whom the writer informs us he noticed at an Ivy League rugby game; an errant kick delivered the ball into her arms, and she nearly fainted after returning it to play. She will not appear in his next book, the writer tells us, because afterward she simply wandered away. Readers familiar with Cheever's educational background—or lack thereof—may wonder if they are to identify him with the narrator of the "Miscellany," whose

Ivy League background is merely implied; the larger question of just who the narrator is, and what his values are, is certainly worth pursuing.

That the authorial voice is both idiosyncratic and cocksure is evident in the second exclusion: "All fat parts for Marlon Brando" (467) are peremptorily dismissed from his future work. So too are all "scornful descriptions" of ugliness or pollution in the American landscape. Cheever's opinion of Marlon Brando is nowhere recorded, and while it is true that he had for many years lavished the best of his descriptive attentions on pleasant urban and suburban settings, it is also true that Cheever was as capable of finding "the worm in the apple" of such scenes as the despised Lawrence Pommeroy—and of describing it with amazing precision when this was appropriate to his thematic purposes. That he would continue to do so up until his final work is beyond dispute; in fact *Oh What a Paradise It Seems* could have taken its inspiration directly from this section of the "Miscellany," since it is Cheever's most direct indictment of the kind of moral corruption that has defaced so much of America's natural beauty.

Again, we can speculate as to whether or not Cheever expects his readers to equate him with the author of this negative manifesto. Can he really assume that we are so naive as to concur in a rejection not of ugliness but of artistic responsibility? A poet might choose to focus attention exclusively on an object of beauty, but a writer of fiction who has committed himself to telling some fundamental truth about a given society cannot long ignore its uglier elements. This brings us full circle, however, to the realization that Cheever's first impulse is always toward "the light," which in some cases means that he willfully overlooks the darkness. Alfred Kazin put it bluntly: "My deepest feeling about Cheever is that his marvelous brightness is an effort to cheer himself up."[43] The facile approach to comforting ourselves, one that we all resort to at times, is simply lying to ourselves by ignoring unpleasant facts or larger truths. Cheever's decision to remove World War II from his first novel, *The Wapshot Chronicle*, may have been just such an effort; he justified it on the grounds that he did not want to confine his subject to a particular epoch, but the effect was to weaken the story's authenticity. Similarly, the almost total avoidance of racial problems and issues in his work (until *Falconer*) raises questions about the seriousness of his commitment as a social observer.

But we should be cautious about taking the manifesto at face value. The writer of fiction has greater freedom than the poet to stand apart from his work, to conceal himself behind his narrator and allow the work to "speak for itself." The author of the "Miscellany" tells us that he intends to avoid all "explicit descriptions of sexual commerce" (something Cheever had managed up to this point but would not hold to consistently in the future), and "all lushes" as well. Yet he immediately launches into a capsule narrative centered on the misfortunes of an alcoholic businessman, complete with family and home in the suburbs, that somehow succeeds in holding our attention and evoking our sympathy even as the author is disclaiming his interest. Indeed this section of the "Miscellany" can be read as a parody of the cold objectivity that was Cheever's entrée into the world of John O'Hara, Dorothy Parker, and other naturalists of the thirties. The unnamed alcoholic returns to his suburban train station at the end of a long day and is greeted by his family; Cheever would be a poor writer (and human being) if he did not expect us to supply a contrary subtext for the following conclusion: "but where is Daddy? It takes two conductors to get him down the stairs. He has lost his hat, his necktie, and his topcoat, and someone has blackened his right eye. He still holds the dispatch case under one arm. No one speaks, no one weeps as they get him into the car and drive him out of our sight, out of our jurisdiction and concern. Out they go, male and female, all the lushes; they throw so little true light on the way we live" (469).

Notice the adjective *true*; Cheever would not deny that heavy drinkers exist—he was arguably one himself at this point. But his surrogate prefers not to write about them, presumably for the same general reason that he would ignore defaced landscapes. These people and things fall short of the best that is in us or that we can aspire to. They are an affront to the noble side of the human spirit. Any attempt by a writer to exclude them from his field of vision, however, can only be seen as ludicrous. It is almost as if a realistic artist like Edward Hopper had suddenly decided, in midcareer, to paint only scenes in which everyone was smiling, out of inner goodness and their sense of the beauty around them. The seeker of light in Cheever might have wanted to write in that mode, but not the seeker after truth.

At this stage of his life, however, Cheever may not have been prepared to be so broad-minded on the subject of the next exclusion in the "Miscellany." The main text here is another brief story showing the harmful effects of a mother's intense affection for her son; presumably this will lead directly to sexual confusion and thence to homosexuality. The link is indisputable, at least to the blindered champion of

59

uncomplicated morality: "He [the son] sits in the sand at her feet, and she runs her fingers through his light hair. Then she does something hideous. One wants to look away, but not before we have seen her undo her pearls and fasten them around his golden neck. 'See how they shine,' says she, doing the clasp as irrevocably as the manacle is welded to the prisoner's shin." (471). Homosexuality is rarely mentioned in Cheever's work prior to *Falconer* (1977), where it is a major element in the narrative; there is ample evidence that as an older man, Cheever fully indulged this side of his identity. The seeming rejection of it as a vice in the Wapshot novels (1957, 1964) suggests that for whatever reason, in the early sixties Cheever was very concerned about the issue and may have been more confused personally on the point than the unequivocal (even Puritanical) voice of the "Miscellany" would have us believe.

In any case, the "Miscellany" presents us with a curious contradiction. The writer claims that he does not want to write about subjects he regards as unpleasant or depressing, but he cannot stop himself from including vignettes exemplifying these people and things. Although he makes it seem that he is having a final fling before moving on to subjects he does like, the very simple-mindedness of the premise opens the door to another view of this fictional essay: Cheever could well be experimenting, tinkering, poking fun at himself and his readers—and perhaps with the whole notion of what a writer should be. As he approached his fiftieth birthday, he had come full circle and was writing stories that were as morally opinionated as "Expelled," his first story, had been. But unlike "Expelled," these stories raise complicated questions that cannot be neatly resolved in a short space. The personal relationships of husbands and wives, parents and children, friends and enemies, admit of so much more shading and variation than the shortcomings of a preparatory school that any attempt to reduce them to a set of commandments would make them the stuff of platitudes. In the "Miscellany," the disorder of real life keeps leaking through the door that the "writer" is attempting to shut against it, and I think Cheever expected the alert reader to notice this.

The final section would seem to support this view. It is more a reminiscence than an exclusion; the author surveys the literary career of "my laconic old friend Royden Blake" (471) and finds it wanting. He divides Blake's work into several periods, but describes it as essentially a plateau of predictable accomplishment starting with moral anecdotes and proceeding to "snobbism" and thence to "his romantic period."

Blake's work, in his friend's opinion, "was characterized by everything that I have mentioned. In his pages one found alcoholics, scarifying descriptions of the American landscape, and fat parts for Marlon Brando" (471). Furthermore, he had lost the ability to evoke "the perfumes of life: sea water, the smoke of burning hemlock, and the breasts of women. He had damaged, you might say, the ear's innermost chamber, where we hear the heavy noise of the dragon's tail moving over the dead leaves" (471).

The line is vintage Cheever, and if any part of the "Miscellany" looks like an artistic credo, this does. The writer describes his final encounter with Blake in a Venetian pensione; the old man is weak, but insists on giving him a detailed outline of his latest story—a narrative centered on the chance meeting of three strangers in an Austrian train station. As the writer listens patiently, Blake sketches his main characters, all of whom have unusual backgrounds or appearances, then suddenly dies without developing them or their situations. The "Miscellany" ends with an enigma, expressed in what seems to be a curt farewell to Blake and writers like him (but one that could have a much wider application): "these were his dying words, and the dying words, it seemed to me, of generations of storytellers, for how could this snowy and trumped-up pass, with its trio of travelers, hope to celebrate a world that lies spread out around us like a bewildering and stupendous dream?" (472).

Royden Blake may be the inferior artist that our author has represented him to be, or he may not (both, after all, are figments of Cheever's imagination). But taken strictly on its own terms, this final line can easily be construed to apply to *all* writers of fiction, whether or not that is the intention of the imaginary writer. Although Cheever himself never published a story quite like this, several of the narratives he set in Europe include chance encounters, and some of his stories are peopled by figures as odd as those dreamed up by Blake. Blake is not alone, then, in his artistic failure. Any creative maker—Daedalus, or Homer, or Hawthorne's "artist of the beautiful," or John Cheever himself—can at best give us only partial glimpses of the reality that surrounds us and of the deeper reality that informs it. Cheever, in short, may be using the persona of his writer-narrator to voice a despairing view of his profession, whether or not he himself believed it. The writer in this light is something of a fool, dealing in illusions not only for his audience, but also for himself. Samuel Johnson once praised Shakespeare (who himself compared poets to madmen) by claiming that he "held a mirror up to nature"; but Cheever's alter ego, if he is that, forces us to notice the crack in the mirror's surface. We know, beyond the possibility of doubt, that Cheever reveled in his craft. But it would be surprising if, as a mature practitioner of that craft, he never doubted either its ultimate value or his own skill.

That he was still capable of writing and publishing a truly inferior story, even at the height of his career, is evident in his next effort, "The Chimera,"[44] published in July 1961. Most of the literary vices and weaknesses that could be detected by a perceptive reader in some of his work of the fifties are here brazenly in full view. The characters in this story of a failed marriage are meant to be comic but prove to be singularly unfunny stereotypes (a henpecked husband, a drunken nag of a wife), their situation is uninteresting, and the theme that evolves from this deadly combination is so thin as to be invisible. Cheever goes as far as to invent a quartet of evil sisters for the wife, all of them apparent murderers of their husbands. The clear implication of all of this is that the husband's life is in danger, and his escape from this marital hell takes the form of a series of dreams in which he is the lover and protector of an equally endangered woman. But the dreams lead nowhere, and the dreamgirl evaporates. The narrator wonders: "Mightn't Olga's going only mean that she was making room for someone else?" (481). The reader of this unequivocal failure can be forgiven for not really caring about stick figures purporting to be characters.

Cheever soon rebounded, however, with "The Brigadier and the Golf Widow,"[45] a well-conceived anatomy of suburban angst in the early sixties. In an interview with Annette Grant published in 1976, Cheever said this story "is about a level of basic anxiety, and the bomb shelter, which places the story at a very particular time, is just a metaphor. . . . that's what I intended anyhow."[46] This was a period marked by increasing fear, for many Americans, of the Soviet Union—an anxiety borne out the following year during the Cuban Missile Crisis, when the world faced its first real nuclear confrontation. President Kennedy had based a major part of his election campaign in 1960 on the assertion that the Soviets held an advantage in the deployment of nuclear missiles, and some frightened Americans rushed to build bomb shelters in their back yards. Always alert to the dark absurdities of life as well as its beauty and light, Cheever—whatever his conscious intention—wrote a tale that delivers the kind of stinging social criticism he would have balked at less than ten years earlier, and the kind that the supposed writer of the "Miscellany" so vehemently decried.

The title characters, we learn in the opening paragraph, have been mislabeled for what appears to be a comic purpose. Mrs. Pastern "would have been known as a golf widow" twenty years earlier, given her husband's obsession with that sport; Charlie Pastern "was brigadier of the [golf] club's locker-room light infantry, and at one time or another declared war on Russia, Czechoslovakia, Yugoslavia and China" (498). His solution to international tensions is simple: "Let's throw a little nuclear hardware at them and show them who's boss" (498). The satiric edge cuts through the narrative meat of the story early enough to indicate Cheever's insistence on its function, and he never stops slicing.

Mrs. Pastern, like her mother and grandmother before her, has a passion of her own: she collects money for worthy causes. The story proper begins when, overburdened by her duties, she presses the "brigadier" into this honorable service. He is assigned to take a contribution from the winsome Mrs. Flannagan, but on discovering that her husband is away, he takes advantage of her charitable nature in another sense. The narrator glides over this transgression with a deceptive blandness, depicting Mr. Pastern as smugly self-assured in his conquest and (despite some serious financial reverses) with his life in general. His seduction of Mrs. Flannagan turns into an affair whose outcome turns on the story's central symbol—a well-equipped bomb shelter the Pasterns have had built on their property. This is the reason for the brigadier's lack of concern about the possible consequences of his personal foreign policy; it also proves to be his undoing.

Before long Mrs. Flannagan has persuaded him to prove his love by giving her his key to the shelter, a fact later discovered by the Pasterns' cleaning woman and eagerly reported by her to Mrs. Pastern. In the midst of this unraveling, Cheever broadens the scope of his criticism of a society tilting toward insanity by having the Pasterns' bishop stop by for a visit, ostensibly on a whim but in fact because he wants to see the shelter. His interest smacks of selfish survivalism and unnerves Mrs. Pastern; thus she is primed for emotional collapse when the cleaning woman telephones: "He [Charlie] had dragged her good name through a hundred escapades, debauched her excellence, and thrown away her love," the omniscient narrator observes, "but she had never imagined that he would betray her in their plans for the end of the world" (507–8). She confronts her husband, who in turn takes out his disillusioned rage on Mrs. Flannagan verbally, but to no avail. The final blow comes when he tries to use the Flannagans' bathroom and comes "face to face with an absolutely naked stranger" (509).

With this shoving of Pastern's nose into his own folly, Cheever leaves little room for doubt or ambiguity about the story's point. The rest of the tale is told rapidly and from a distance, in a letter from the unnamed narrator's mother, read by him some time later. In it he learns that Mr. Pastern has been sent to prison for grand larceny, that his wife and son are living in the Bronx, and that his daughter has left college to find a job. The Flannagans have divorced. The letter and story end with a distressing glimpse of Mrs. Flannagan making an unannounced visit to the Pasterns' former home, and more particularly to the once lovely garden whose statuary and layout hide the underground bomb shelter. She is finally ordered off the property by a maid.

This scene and the exposition of Mrs. Pastern's plight are perhaps the only moments of the story that engage our sympathies, and in both cases it can be argued that the brigadier's women deserve their punishments. In any event, the story is not primarily concerned with sympathetic responses. It depicts what Cheever saw as inhuman behavior, and if the satirical fictions of Jonathan Swift are any guide, the blending of exaggerated action and flat characters, skillfully worked with touches of realism, can both amuse and instruct readers. Cheever deserves credit, in this instance, for doing what he had sometimes failed to do: allowing his self-destructive characters to self-destruct rather than saving their skins at the last moment. Following his confrontation with Mrs. Flannagan, Pastern returns home, unfurls a newspaper and repeats his call for a nuclear attack on the nation's enemies. Then in a startling flash of insight, his wife cuts directly to the core of his disease: "You *want* the world to end, don't you? Don't you, Charlie, don't you? I've known it all along, but I couldn't admit it to myself, it seemed so ruthless—but then one learns something new every day" (510).

This story appeared three years before John Aldridge's stinging criticism of Cheever's penchant for easy resolutions, and if it is an exception to the pattern of happy resolutions that does exist in many of Cheever's tales, it is a notable one. The fact that the story's moment of truth is reserved for a woman, and a wife, should also be recognized.

Cheever was working on his second novel, *The Wapshot Scandal*, in the early sixties, and several of the stories he published in those years

The Dream Unravels

are excerpts from that book. Any feminist studying the thematic content of his work during this period would have to conclude, even on the basis of the novel alone, that Cheever's skepticism concerning the emergence of the new, "active" woman still ran very deep. And there is additional evidence that while he was capable of creating intelligent female characters who could occasionally surmount the difficulties of their lives, he apparently detested women who not only overcame male domination but went on to dominate and, in his view, destroy their families. He had given fullest expression to this theme in *The Wapshot Chronicle,* and he returned to it with a vengeance in "An Educated American Woman" (1963).[47]

The woman of that title is Jill Chidchester Madison, who has pursued her interest in French literature past college graduation and into her marriage with Georgie Madison, whom she describes in a note for her alumnae magazine as "an unintellectual 190-pound halfback" (521). The narrator, who reserves final judgment on his characters until the story's end, insists that Jill is not "aggressive," merely able and charming; it is her finer qualities that account for her successes both in literature (a publisher is interested in her biography of Flaubert, although brief quotations from the work in progress establish the inferiority of her writing beyond question) and in local civic causes.

Like many of Cheever's dangerous women, then, Jill is an activist. Within the narrative terms set by Cheever, that automatically means that her personal priorities are wrongheaded, like those of Grandmother Delancey and Aunt Louisa in "The Lowboy." For a woman who gives herself over to social causes will not, in this view, have sufficient concern for her own family's needs, and the family will suffer as a result; all of which is a clear perversion of the natural order of things. This line of reasoning—it is actually the story's theme—is borne out in "An Educated American Woman," but in a strangely inverted fashion. In effect, Cheever hides behind a purportedly feminist (but apparently male) narrator who tells a tale that unequivocally indicts Jill for the death of the Madisons' son, then sneers at Georgie's ineffectuality when that story ends.

Cheever tips his thematic hand quite early by giving careful attention to Jill's upbringing—actually her moral ruination—at the hands of her widowed mother. Mrs. Chidchester, the writer of "seventeen unpublished books," had been obsessed with the idea of Jill's brilliance and its furthering, to the point of ruling out any preparation in more mundane skills. She learned French but never washed the dishes.

65

Her husband accepts this as factual background—he really has no other choice—but is deeply puzzled, and troubled, by its results:

> She had been raised as an intellectual, her emancipation was still questioned in many quarters, and since he seemed to possess more latitude, to hold a stronger traditional position, it was his place to yield on matters like housework. It was not her choice, he knew, that she was raised as an intellectual, but the choice, having been made by others, seemed irrevocable. His restless sexual nature attributed to her softness, warmth, and the utter darkness of love; but why, he wondered as he polished the forks, did there seem to be some contradiction between these attributes and the possession of a clear mind? (528)

In short, Georgie can both admire Jill's intellectual gifts and (as he does) become enraged when she interrupts their lovemaking with an idea—stated in French, of course—for her book on Flaubert. Eventually he finds consolation in the arms of an older woman.

The problem comes to a head when, in the middle of Jill's campaign to prevent the construction of an unnecessary and aesthetically destructive highway, the Madisons' son Bibber becomes ill. Georgie, who has attempted to arrange child care during Jill's frequent absences, returns home one afternoon to find Bibber feverish and bleeding at the mouth. This time, in contrast to his choice of outcomes in "The Trouble of Marcie Flint," Cheever allows the child to die, but the point of this decision seems obvious and less commendable than in the earlier story, precisely because it is so programmatic. Cheever is not in this instance asking us to extend our sympathies to anyone: he is killing off one character so that we will be compelled to point the finger of blame at another. Lest even the densest of readers miss the point, the narrator reports that when Jill wires her mother in Florence, asking to visit her, she is answered with an airy, artsy rejection. Mrs. Chidchester explains to her daughter that she has "come to a time of life when I do not especially like to dwell upon the subject of passing away" (535).

Georgie and Jill divorce and pursue their separate careers. Georgie blames Jill for Bibber's death, but the storyteller ends by observing "how inferior" Georgie was to Jill, "how immature" (535). Given the stacked evidence, however, the weight of heaviest censure must fall on Jill's shoulders. Georgie's only sin is his uxoriousness, the sin of Adam: he was too willing to accept his wife's assertion of self as a prime value, and too unwilling to assert the older, more traditional system of values that would have kept her in the home and available for emergencies like the one that claimed their son's life. The serious implications of this point make it impossible to dismiss the story as representing just one more turn in the path of Cheever's developing consciousness concerning the war between the sexes. The fact of Bibber Madison's death proclaims the opposite: Jill Madison and "women like her" are meant to be seen as an abomination. If Cheever ever wrote a story that deliberately distorts female sense and sensibility in the name of traditional values, this is it.

After "The Enormous Radio" Cheever's most famous short story is the mysterious tale "The Swimmer,"[48] made popular by a moderately successful 1966 film. Thus far, few film adaptations of Cheever's work have been able to convey his peculiar combination of fantasy and realism; it is not surprising that a narrative as original as "The Swimmer" suffers somewhat in translation. Published in 1964, this story comes closer to mythologizing the outward signs and inner turmoil of suburban life than any other by Cheever. Its protagonist, Neddy Merrill, is instantly recognizable as a member of the same unhappy crew that Cash Bentley, Johnny Hake, and Francis Weed had earlier joined: the disaffected males of Cheever's suburbia, lost souls tortured by their unsatisfying existence in earthly paradise. More decisively than any of his previous tales, "The Swimmer" asserts that the spiritual gap between paradise and suburbia was indeed wide and growing larger. This seems to be the point of casting the story as a backyard tour of several hamlets, and of choosing the swimming pool as a central symbol.

Like his fictional brothers, Neddy Merrill drinks more heavily than he should, although he is first pictured as something of an athlete. The story's introduction, a deceptively comic chorus, mocks the mindless protestations of the prosperous against their own weakness on this score: "'I *drank* too much,' said Donald Westerhazy. 'We all *drank* too much,' said Lucinda Merrill. 'It must have been the wine,' said Helen Westerhazy, 'I *drank* too much of that claret'" (603). Against this background chorus, we see Neddy sitting beside the Westerhazys' pool, one hand in the water, the other holding a glass of gin.

Starting from nothing more substantial than a slightly alcoholic impulse, Neddy sets out on an eight-mile cross-country journey, inventing "the Lucinda River," a chain of friends' swimming pools, as he goes. His near-marathon traverses several communities (it appears to begin in Shady Hill and end in Bullet Park, where the Merrills live) and, as it happens, a fair number of social gatherings. Along the way Neddy surprises and occasionally offends several friends, but most of them welcome him and ply him with drinks.

A generally overlooked weakness of the story is Cheever's refusal to open up Neddy's consciousness for the reader to any great extent. This reticence is essential, perhaps, to its shock ending, but also unfair to the reader. If we are finally to discover that Neddy's personal problems are much more serious than the events of the story had indicated, we deserve some advance warning in the form of insights provided by Neddy; but such hints are scarce and slight. In his interview with Annette Grant, Cheever admitted that the story was "terribly difficult . . . to write," adding, "I couldn't ever show my hand. Night was falling, the year was dying. It wasn't a question of technical problems, but one of imponderables. When he finds it's dark and cold, it has to have happened. And, by God, it did happen. I felt dark and cold for some time after I finished that story" (62).

As Neddy leaves the Westerhazys and his wife, the narrator informs us simply that "Making his way home by an uncommon route gave him the feeling that he was a pilgrim, an explorer, a man with a destiny, and he knew that he would find friends all along the way; friends would line the banks of the Lucinda River" (604). This upbeat mood is sustained through the first half of Neddy's trip. Cheever harmonizes atmosphere and events into a rhapsodic narrative poem in this section, but what we are hearing is a siren's song: "Oh, how bonny and lush were the banks of the Lucinda River! Prosperous men and women gathered by the sapphire-colored waters while caterer's men in white coats passed them cold gin" (605). Neddy would join them but is impelled by a sense of mission. He has to get home, so he confines his socializing to greetings and gratitude when invited to refresh himself. Then, at roughly the midpoint of his journey, his world starts to come apart.

To underscore the change, Cheever emphasizes water imagery in his descriptions; it seems that both the medium of Neddy's journey and the heavens above answer to the emptiness inside him. When he arrives at the Levys', he finds that their home and pool are deserted. He sees around him only the detritus of a recent party and watches the formation of storm clouds overhead. The prospect of rain cheers rather than disheartens him, however, and he waits out the storm in the Levys' gazebo before moving on to his next pool. This involves crossing an intervening riding circle; Neddy is surprised, when he arrives

The Dream Unravels

there, to discover that the ring has fallen into disuse. This outward deterioration hints at an internal decay that has no name, both in Neddy and his environment. Similarly, at his next stop, the pool has been drained and a For Sale sign posted. Apparently *unlike* some of Cheever's early "Chekhovian" characters, Neddy starts to doubt his memory and wonders if he is not distorting his sense of reality by deliberately ignoring unpleasant realities. At this juncture he is forced to cross a highway, a "point of no return." Waiting for the traffic to thin out, he becomes an object of ridicule, and someone throws a beer can at him. If the metaphorical nature of Neddy's swim has been vaguely realized thus far, Cheever now asserts it more forcefully—even as he leaves the metaphor itself open to wider interpretation: "He could not go back, he could not even recall with any clearness the green water at the Westerhazys', the sense of inhaling the day's components, the friendly and relaxed voices saying that they had *drunk* too much. In the space of an hour, more or less, he had covered a distance that made his return impossible" (607).

Perhaps remembering a scene from his first suburban story, "Roseheath," Cheever lightens the somber mood of this section as Neddy arrives at the Hallorans' pool. Mr. and Mrs. Halloran, an older couple, are "zealous reformers" ("but they were not Communists," the narrator assures us) and swim in the nude. As a "polite" gesture, Neddy takes off his trunks before joining them. Then just as quickly as it had turned brighter, the narrative tone darkens. Mrs. Halloran proffers her regrets at the "misfortunes" afflicting Neddy—misfortunes the reader has so far heard nothing about, including the sale of the home he is swimming toward. As she starts to mention his "poor children," Ned interrupts, apparently to correct her, and the reader might easily guess that Mrs. Halloran, not Neddy, has the faulty memory. She relents, and after expressing his gratitude Neddy goes on to the Biswangers, social climbers that he imagines will welcome him eagerly. Instead Mrs. Biswanger snubs him, and this time he has to ask for a drink. By now he is so worn down he needs the liquor to mask his physical fatigue, but he is determined to complete his mission.

His next stop is at the home and pool of a former mistress, and their curt exchange tells us a great deal more about Neddy than the narrator has previously revealed:

"What do you want?" she asked.
"I'm swimming across the county."

69

"Good Christ. Will you ever grow up?"

"What's the matter?"

"If you've come here for money," she said, "I won't give you another cent."

"You could give me a drink."

"I could but I won't. I'm not alone."

"Well, I'm on my way." (611)

And so the pieces of the puzzle start to fit together. Mrs. Halloran was right, and so was Neddy when he worried about the accuracy of his memory. The countless drinks along the way are part of a larger pattern of willful oblivion, repressing problems so troubling that they cannot be raised to the surface of consciousness. We now see that like the Chekhovian characters Cheever had delineated in the thirties, Neddy Merrill has in fact chosen to lose touch with the truth rather than to suffer under its crushing weight. But in "The Swimmer" Cheever uses extended fantasy, and more particularly a metaphorical action, to instruct his readers concerning the psychological costs of such a strategy—something he would not have attempted as a younger writer on the rise. And because the instruction is implied rather than stated (a characteristic of Cheever's best work), it is all the more forceful. As he leaves his mistress's property, Neddy looks at the sky, which has darkened with the onset of night, and "seems" to see Andromeda, Cepheus, and Cassiopeia—the constellations of winter. For the first time in his adult life, he starts to cry.

Hardly able to swim the length of the two remaining pools, at last Neddy arrives at his own home to find it dark and deserted: "He shouted, pounded on the door, tried to force it with his shoulder, and then, looking in at the windows, saw that the place was empty" (612).

Even readers alert enough to have anticipated this kind of ending may be stunned by the cold emptiness of the story's final scene. Yet it is perfectly consistent with the reticence the narrator has maintained throughout his story, and more justified than his earlier blotting out of Neddy's consciousness. The story's opening seems no less misleading in light of what we have seen and come to understand during Neddy's "progress" from boozy cheerfulness to the edge of the void; yet we can believe, finally, that he hadn't much in the way of enlightenment to share in the first place. The significant part of his identity—the part that needed a good, long swim in the waters that stretch from one end of his world to the other—was simply too banal for words, too deeply stained for any water to cleanse.

Such Stuff as Dreams Are Made On

Relatively late in his career—in the mid-1960s—Cheever had established himself as a novelist and tended to think of himself as one. He continued to write short stories but was increasingly drawn toward the writing of "novel segments" or chapters of longer works that could be excerpted for publication in the *New Yorker* and other magazines. *The Wapshot Chronicle* had been a notable success, and although *The Wapshot Scandal* disappointed many critics, its appearance seemed to demonstrate that Cheever was capable of sustained work on major themes. In both novels he had examined (although somewhat disjointedly) family relationships damaged by individual and societal inanities; here was the work of his apprenticeship as a short story writer writ large, and he seemed finally to be following the proper career pattern for a "successful" writer. He had, after all, yearned to be a novelist almost from the beginning.[49]

Inevitable as this change was, in purely artistic terms it may have been a mistake. Cheever was right in determining that novels would earn more money for himself and his family, along with greater professional recognition. Thanks in part to television and a general decline in literacy, the short story form in America had itself entered a period of decline. But a novel that became a best-seller opened a path to additional revenues, and motion picture rights were among the most lucrative of these. In fact, Hollywood producers were for a time very interested in the Wapshot novels and paid Cheever a respectable $75,000 for the rights to them.[50] Still, one can only imagine what wonders Cheever might have been able to perform as a master of the short story, if ambition and such financial concerns had not turned his creative energies in another direction. His highly productive youth was behind him, but as *Falconer* and his final stories would demonstrate, his creativity had not deserted him. And there is ample evidence that while he was an artificial novelist, he was a natural teller of short stories.

Personal as well as professional concerns must be taken into account in assessing this phase of Cheever's work. Biographer Scott Donaldson has provided clear verification of Cheever's gradual descent into alco-

71

holism, his marital infidelities and indiscretions, and the tensions that afflicted the Cheever home in Ossining. Donaldson also shows that Cheever could be both circumspect and loving as a husband and father, yet the clear impression one receives from his analysis, from Susan Cheever's memoir, and from the numerous interviews given by a "reformed" Cheever in later years, is that the personal demons he had managed to subdue as a younger man proved incorrigible after he turned fifty.

When his third novel, *Bullet Park* (1969), appeared it was demolished in a *New York Times* review by Benjamin DeMott.[51] Other reviews were more favorable, but the prominence of the *Times* piece meant lower book sales as well as a devastating blow to Cheever's ego. The gamble he had taken in committing himself to longer fiction had apparently failed. Eventually he would reverse his slide into failure and self-abasement with the writing of *Falconer,* but in 1969 the enthusiastic reception of this novel was far in the future, whereas the evidence of rejection was, to him at least, close at hand.

It would be simplistic, however, to identify a single event as the main cause of a trend that had long been developing. As we have seen, Cheever's cynical view of American society—an attitude that had its roots in both the Depression thirties and Roaring Twenties—was a matter of record. He was equally despairing about the writer's role in what he saw as a deeply flawed culture. A steady undercurrent of pessimism runs through many of his short stories extending back to "Expelled" and continuing almost to the end of his life. Even in those tales where the reader can take comfort in a last-minute reprieve for an endangered protagonist, or a lyrically phrased assurance that the sun will rise again tomorrow, there is often a lingering sense that, on balance, humankind is a sorry lot. This odor of despair rises from story after story, whether the central characters are exceptional or ordinary. And although it may reek of stale liquor, its essence is not chemical.

A major story from what might be called this "late mature" period, "The World of Apples" (1966)[52] is one of a handful by Cheever directly or indirectly concerned with writing and writers ("A Miscellany . . . ," "An Educated American Woman," and "The Jewels of the Cabots" are others). In this case the writer is Asa Bascomb, an aging poet from New England who has settled in Italy. Cheever makes good use of his experiences during an extended stay in Italy in 1956–57, enriching his story with plenty of local color. But the function of this brushwork is different here from its purpose in several other narratives based on his

Italian sabbatical. Bascomb, a still lively eighty-two at the time of the story, confronts a form of psychic deterioration that threatens to drive him mad; as counterpoint, Cheever's depiction of Italian scenes provides a welcome contrast to this interior struggle. While taking a pleasant walk in the woods one day, the poet inadvertently happens upon a pair of lovers. The scene, for all its bucolic innocence, triggers an obsession with pornographic and scatological images; and it is Bascomb's powerful poetic sensibility, ironically, that almost destroys his spirit. This is a story about art framed in starkly human terms, and it raises disturbing questions about the role of sexuality, as one form of beauty, in life as well as art. The challenge of treating material so inherently difficult with the proper balance of effects is greater here than in most of his stories, but Cheever answers it. Bascomb never becomes a fool, and ultimately he is able to save himself.

Once again the temptation to see Cheever making himself the centerpiece of his story is strong. But he was almost thirty years younger than Bascomb in 1966, and the old master is more reminiscent of Ezra Pound—or much more likely a composite born of Cheever's imagination. In a way, however, Cheever is a part of Bascomb. Early on, the narrator tells us that "Bascomb believed, as Cocteau once said, that the writing of poetry was the exploitation of a substratum of memory that was imperfectly understood" (615); this is a view that Cheever himself applied to fiction.[53] Add to this the points that Cheever, like his expatriate poet, had been lionized in the Soviet Union[54] and that they both claim a New England heritage, and the resemblance becomes more pronounced. Yet the central point remains: this story is meant to anatomize the artistic temperament undergoing terrible stress. Asa Bascomb, if he represents someone or something other than himself, could symbolize all creative artists made vulnerable to psychological breakdown by their own humanity.

Bascomb does nothing to deserve the spiritual pain he is forced to endure. Like many accomplished artists he is vain, and his vanity questions the wisdom of Nobel committees that have denied him their prize. But his soul is expansive, and his native generosity leads him to welcome countless tourists eager for a glimpse of him. One of Cheever's masterstrokes in "The World of Apples" is the effective juxtaposing of such encounters, in which the poet meets a young married couple or some nuns from a Roman convent, with passages revealing his descent into harrowing obscenity: "On the next day he wrote The Confessions of A Public School Headmaster. He burned the manuscript at noon. As he came sadly down the stairs onto his terrace he found there fourteen students from the University of Rome who, as soon as he appeared, began to chant 'The Orchards of Heaven'—the opening sonnet in *The World of Apples*" (618), Bascomb's most famous work.

The poet is tortured both by his shame at having his talent perverted to the level of pornography and his awareness that as a pornographer he is second rate: he has nothing new to contribute to the genre. In an effort to cleanse his mind through contact with great art and music he flees to Rome, only to find himself confronted by a male prostitute. Later, in a concert hall, he cannot stop himself from mentally undressing a beautiful soprano. There is genuine sadness in all of this, but Cheever also brings his gift for comic absurdity to these scenes. We can smile—however ruefully—at the tricks Bascomb's mind plays on him, yet the reality of his torment is always before us. Bascomb's best poetry, like some of Cheever's best stories, had thrived on the loveliness of nature and humanity. Now the imaginative power that re-created those beauties in verse languishes in a spiritual pigsty, and the poet cannot dream his way out of the mire.

After several days and nights of anguish, a seemingly chance remark by his maid points the way to a possible escape. She claims that a carved angel, "the sacred angel of Monte Giordano," has the power to "cleanse the thoughts of a man's heart" (620). Desperate, Bascomb takes a gold medal awarded him by the Soviet government and sets out on foot to find the angel's shrine.

On the way to Monte Giordano he stops for a rest and falls asleep; then magically, the quality of his interior life changes for the better. In a dream he sees an old man performing an act of simple kindness, giving a bone to a stray dog. Awakened by the sound of thunder, Bascomb resumes his hike and encounters—a stray dog. The animal is frightened by the approaching storm, and Bascomb strokes its head. As the storm moves closer, they find a lean-to occupied by another old man, who invites them in. Bascomb studies his host enviously: "he seemed to have reached an organic peace of mind that Bascomb coveted" (621). The man smiles and peruses a stamp album as the storm hits. He may lack poetic sensibility, Bascomb decides, but he seems invulnerable to the suffering that such sensitivity is heir to. The rain falls, the dog whines, and Bascomb pets him.

If a short story could adequately address tragic issues, this moment—so reminiscent of King Lear sitting in a hovel on a storm-wracked heath—could well serve as a moment of tragic recognition for Bascomb, opening out as it does to the possibility of spiritual rebirth through suffering. Wisely, Cheever refrains from attempting to force Bascomb into a role too large for his character. When the rain stops, Bascomb, refreshed, resumes his walk to the church at Monte Giordano.

As he had anticipated, the church's priest expects a token of sincerity before allowing him to enter. Bascomb is nonplussed to learn that his Lermontov medal falls short on two counts, its communist origin and its lack of a hallmark. Once again, however, something wonderful happens: the clouds part and a ray of sunshine strikes the medal. Impressed, the priest makes the sign of the cross and admits Bascomb to the angel's chapel, where he places the medal at the angel's feet and prays: "God bless Walt Whitman. God bless Hart Crane. God bless Dylan Thomas. God bless William Faulkner, Scott Fitzgerald, and especially Ernest Hemingway" (622).

Hemingway would have scoffed at that sunbeam, but Cheever almost makes it plausible as a fitting talisman (together with the medal) marking the end of Bascomb's ordeal. What is undeniable is the need, if the story is to avoid catastrophe, for some form of intervention—an imposition that may be seen as either supernatural or natural in terms of the story's events, but that must ultimately be regarded as authorial. God was asleep, and Cheever either woke him up or parted those clouds himself.

Interestingly, only three of the literary saints in the poet's pantheon are fellow poets. The final three are writers of fiction, and this supports the view that Bascomb is partially Cheever, whether or not he wants us to think so. Perhaps a more telling point is that the litany celebrates gifted creators hounded by serious personal difficulties, great artists who struck Faustian bargains that brought them fame at the expense of contentment. The themes of sexual maladjustment and alcoholic dissipation run like troubled streams through their lives. If Bascomb speaks for Cheever, his voice is heavy with compassion.

That night the poet sleeps peacefully, and on his return home he starts to write a long poem "on the inalienable dignity of light and air that, while it would not get him the Nobel Prize, would grace the last months of his life" (623). The line is prophetic: in the last years of his own life, Cheever would exercise his declining powers on the writing of a novella, *Oh What a Paradise It Seems*, which warns of the polluting encroachments of modern civilization on the gifts of nature.

Strangely enough, as his personal life went into a tailspin, the narrative voice in many of Cheever's stories became more assertive, if rather petulant at the prospect of a world gone haywire. And it seems equally strange that during a time when America became mired in the Vietnam War, and when such domestic issues as civil rights and political chicanery at the highest levels of government continued to dominate much of the public consciousness, Cheever rarely tried to connect such concerns with the material of his short fiction. He may have returned to his belief that locating his stories in a particular time or political context diminished their significance. Throughout his life he had been exploring questions more complex than those posed by newspaper headlines, in places that journalists usually overlook. Still, the absence of discernible connections between his characters' lives and more humdrum pressures than those represented by the seven deadly sins is puzzling, if not disappointing.

Occasionally, flashes of lightning break across the evening sky of these years, piercing the haze of alcoholism that Cheever had allowed to weaken his native talent and acquired skill. For the most part his greatest stories had been told, however. The best of his later writing is often to be found squirreled away in anecdotes or miniatures—parts of story-groups loosely held together under a single heading, rather than unified in a conventional sense. His more conventional stories from these years ("Percy," "The Fourth Alarm," and "Artemis, the Honest Well Digger," for example), are disturbingly misogynistic and sometimes lapse into medium-core pornography reminiscent of Asa Bascomb's obscene daydreams—something Cheever had earlier tried to avoid. The temper of the times was increasingly permissive, and he may have felt that changing his approach to sexuality was not only justified but necessary. The disorder of his personal life may have been a factor in the change as well. Not surprisingly, his forays into this strange new world lack authority, and in their awkwardness tend to confirm the wisdom of his earlier reticence.

"The Jewels of the Cabots" (1972)[55] attempts to combine the "collection" format that would later be used less effectively in such narratives as "Three Stories" (1973) and "The Leaves, The Lion-Fish, and the Bear" (1974) with a distinctly antinostalgic return to St. Botolphs. In large part the story is about the narrator himself; he does not identify himself by name, but he includes certain Cheevers on a list of "wrong" branches of patrician families, along with the Cabots of his title. As in

so many vintage Cheever stories, and following the instruction he gave
to his own writing classes, the opening snaps the reader to attention:
"Funeral services for the murdered man were held in the Unitarian
church in the little village of St. Botolphs." Then the focus abruptly
shifts from the murder victim, Amos Cabot, to the storyteller and his
relationship with the family, and especially the Cabot women. Mrs.
Cabot, the narrator recalls, was a strict moralist of the old New England
variety who lectured students at the local academy on the evils of drink
and tobacco but saw nothing of earthly vanity in her own taste for ex-
pensive diamond rings. The memory of her intolerance sparks another,
equally unpleasant recollection for the narrator; he sadly relates a series
of anti-Semitic remarks by his mother, who incredibly had never realized that her son's father-in-law was Jewish (as was John Cheever's).

The "aside" seems accidental, yet by underscoring St. Botolphs'
(sic) provincialism it serves to bolster the story's main theme. Unfortunately this effort at cohesiveness is atypical. The narrative flow is
frequently broken by abrupt (or nonexistent) transitions, as when the
storyteller shifts his attention to young Molly Cabot as he remembers
her, "a lovely young woman with a sleepy look that was quickly dis-
pelled by a brilliant smile" (684). Her image brightens his reverie, but
only temporarily. In short order we learn that Molly has a half-brother
(her mother's child by an earlier marriage) that she prefers to keep
hidden because he is a hydrocephalic dwarf, and still another brother,
her father's illegitimate son. Literally then, the jewels of the story's
title are Mrs. Cabot's, but metaphorically each facet of the Cabots'
miserable life as a family emerges as a kind of flawed jewel for the
reader's scrutiny. Molly's sister Geneva at first has an ambiguous status
in the family portrait; that changes—but only slightly—when she steals
her mother's jewelry and runs away to Africa. The disposition of the
narrative's *moral* gems is more complicated.

Because of the narrator's earlier involvement with Molly, any pre-
tense at total objectivity in his account of things is out of the question.
Instead, subjective emotion becomes a dominant feature of the story's
telling, threatening to explode its already fragile structure. But whereas
that is precisely what happened in Cheever's earliest stories, before his
conversion to naturalism, here passion seems to have cooled to the
degree that at any given point, the reader can easily grasp what is being
said. The narrative focus changes often enough, however, and so rapidly, that some confusion about the story's larger aims is likely on a first

reading. Compounding the problem is the fact that the Cabots and their follies are only part of the tale.

Geneva's theft precipitates a violent argument between her parents. Mr. Cabot leaves to move in with his mistress, but later returns because "He was worried about Molly, and in such a small place there were appearances to be considered" (692). His decision is based on a convenient mixture of sensitivity and hypocrisy and leads directly to his death. His wife decides to poison him with arsenic, and she succeeds. Following Cabot's death, his mistress, realizing what has happened, tries to bring Mrs. Cabot to justice. She is dissuaded by a local judge who clearly prefers to keep the whole matter quiet—as decorously quiet as the existence of Molly's brothers, and the myriad of family horrors tucked away in the dusty closets and selective memories of St. Botolphs.

In his Wapshot novels, Cheever had made a valiant effort to exorcise the devils of his neo-Puritanical upbringing by inventing a fictional region peopled by emotionally stunted characters. Ironically, however, he had sketched into his background a gallery of characters so grotesque—Aunt Justina in the *Chronicle* is a prime example—that they are almost charming in a Dickensian manner. "The Jewels of the Cabots" is sufficiently compact, and certainly caustic enough in its outlook, to make the same thematic point without the distracting background clutter. St. Botolphs in this telling is a dirty place, and not just because it is old and decaying. The people who live here simply prefer to hide their wickedness, which has nothing to do with ordinary pleasure and everything to do with a refusal to love, to accept one another as they are, to show compassion for the weakest among them. The real heroine of the story is the "bad" daughter Geneva, who eventually marries an Egyptian army officer and settles into a life of harmless decadence. The narrator happily visits her in Luxor, and after a pleasant (if heavily alcoholic) week there, he too severs all ties with the Cabots.

Besides serving as a hardbitten farewell to St. Botolphs, the story is noteworthy for its problematic insistence on the narrator's presence. As both a participant in his story and a critic of his writing, he is so much in the foreground as to be something of a nuisance. He interrupts his own account of Molly's parents' breakup to discourse at considerable length on his tendency to gloss over life's rougher seams, to highlight more pleasant things: "Children drown, beautiful women are mangled in automobile accidents, cruise ships founder, and men die lingering deaths in mines and submarines, but you will find none of this in my accounts. In the last chapter the ship comes home to port, the children are saved, the miners will be rescued. Is this an infirmity of the genteel or a conviction that there are discernible moral truths?" (688).

Without answering the question directly, he goes on to cite instances (one of them set in Rome) of unpleasant "facts" of life—tawdry, nasty scenes sprinkled with profane snatches of dialogue—that fall short of the *truth* as he sees it. His intention, he tells us, is to compose an edition of the *New York Times* filled with nothing but good news. The story of the Cabots is a mere footnote to this, his real work.

This may be Cheever's sarcastic response to those critics, Alfred Kazin and John Aldridge among them, who regard him as a Pollyanna, an avoider of unpleasant implications. In simple terms, "The Jewels of the Cabots" bears out their verdict—at least as far as Geneva is concerned—but we should recall that the sordidness of the Cabots' lives and Mr. Cabot's death are not hidden from view. Even Geneva's successful escape is tainted: she has gotten grossly overweight in exile. These are not mere distractions or sidelights. Taken all together they seem to constitute the point of the story. As with "A Miscellany of Characters That Will Not Appear," the stuff of the narrative tends to subvert the writer's proclaimed intention to simplify life; once more it is necessary to distinguish Cheever from the teller of his tale. While the ersatz "good news" edition of the *Times* never saw the light of day, this enigmatic "footnote" of a story did. Light and darkness mingle disconcertingly in this tale, but their union produces something astonishingly like truth.

Despite his persistent longing to discover and revel in life's blessings, Cheever's descent into a personal hell accelerated in 1973 and 1974. He developed serious heart trouble, possibly brought on by his heavy drinking.[56] In 1974 he accepted a teaching assignment in Boston, but became progressively less able to meet his classroom obligations. He had started another novel about prison life, only to find he was unable to write with anything approaching consistency. He had hit bottom.

The self-destructiveness of this period is mirrored in a story published a year after Cheever submitted to a rigorous drying out in a New York clinic. "The President of the Argentine" (1976)[57] describes the lunatic behavior of a drunken old writer who wanders the streets of Boston, reaching out desperately to passersby for companionship. Love, or the possibility of finding it, has long since flown from his life, and he amuses himself by trying to put a hat on a statue near Commonwealth Avenue, until a policeman objects. It is the story's introduction, however, that offers the most intimate glimpse of Cheever as a writer so worn down by life that he is unable to pursue his craft. The narrator—and he is essentially Cheever—lists several aborted attempts at story beginnings, then confides:

> Here endeth my stab at yesterday's fiction. No one's been reading it for forty years. It went out with easel painting, and by easel painting one means the sort of painting that used to be displayed on easels. Two curates playing checkers by a cockatoo's roost. Painting has cast off its frames, and yet one deeply misses the massive and golden celebrations—fruit and angels—for their element of ultimate risk. By framing a painting the artist, of course, declared it to be a distillate of his deepest feelings about love and death. By junking the frame he destroyed the risk of a declaration. He may, as he will claim, have opened doors, porticos, gates, and mountain passes onto an unframed infinity of comprehension; or he may merely have displayed his abysmal lack of vitality. . . . and my account of putting a hat on a statue is frameless and may indeed not deserve a frame at all. (43)

Beneath the obvious self-pity of this confession can be heard an uncompromising self-indictment, delivered by a writer who realizes he is (or was) at a low ebb. His concern extends beyond matters of form considered for their own sake, into the underworld of the soul, where forms—or "frames" in this case—are selected unconsciously for later conscious fashioning. When that region is in disarray, creative work cannot even begin.

The story of Cheever's physical recovery has been amply documented. Following his stay at the Smithers Clinic, he gave up drinking and was able to return to serious work on *Falconer*. With the help of large-scale media attention, primarily from *Newsweek* magazine,[58] this fourth novel rode a wave of public and critical approval that would reestablish Cheever's literary reputation in a way that exemplifies the best and the worst values in contemporary American life. *Falconer* (1976) proved that Cheever had recovered professionally as well as personally from the failure of *Bullet Park;* in telling the story of Ezekiel Farragut, a jailed WASP who has lost his moral bearings but fashions a new, stronger identity in prison, Cheever also managed to reverse his stance on homosexuality, and to depict the seamiest facets of prison life with surprising authority. He had gained second-hand knowledge of this underworld as a writing instructor in Sing Sing prison, near his home in Ossining.

As beneficial as this success was for Cheever, it only served to reinforce the view that his contribution to American letters should be evaluated primarily in terms of his work as a novelist. Some of his short stories continued to be read and taught, and scholars would occasionally call attention to the fact that he had published more than 170 short stories, most of them in leading magazines; but the obvious implications of that imbalance would tend to go unnoticed.

With the publication of *The Stories of John Cheever* in 1978, this tendency should have been reversed. An oddly biased editorial decision, however, has had the unintended result of greatly complicating any attempt at comprehensive assessment. Cheever and his editors apparently concurred in the view that nothing he had written prior to 1947 was worth including in this retrospective collection. Cheever's right to his claim that the earlier stories were "immature" is indisputable; yet common sense would suggest that out of seventy-five of these, a few might be good enough to replace some of those in the anthology, which in any case does not appear to have been rigorously selective in its selection of post-1947 stories. But writers are frequently not the best judges of their own work, and the appearance of this collection must at the very least be credited with partially restoring a sense of perspective to critical analyses of Cheever's accomplishments.

Cheever wrote his last short story, "The Island,"[59] in 1981. Following his literary comeback, he had enjoyed several years of public and critical recognition, but his body could not recover from the punishment he had so consistently given it prior to 1975. Although he continued to accommodate the public's demand for personal appearances and the academics' requests for information, he had begun to die, a victim of cancer. "The Island" would be followed in 1982 by a novella, *Oh What a Paradise It Seems*, but the short story is a more fitting coda to its author's life work. More of a fantasized reverie than a story, it is not one of Cheever's best imaginative tales; as a farewell to his art, however, it is both affecting and revelatory. In setting and tone it harkens back to Shakespeare's farewell to his profession, *The Tempest*, a play that Cheever knew well.

Fantasy in this final tale becomes a device for examining its own value in relation to realism. Cheever first conjures up an idealized world, then creates a troupe of spirits to people it; their very existence establishes the theme of the story. The storyteller arrives on the island aboard "Harry Morton's little two-motor Fokker" (41), which has been forced down with engine trouble. He is one of a group traveling from Nassau to a friend's home "in the Lesser Antilles." As with Prospero's magic island, this noplace is situated in a vaguely defined area, somewhere near the Bermuda triangle. If we doubt its existence, the narrator, himself pleasantly mystified, seems blithely unaware of either our skepticism or the dreamlike sound of his voice as he escorts us around the island.

The place is unmistakably paradise as Cheever would have it, the final home of once-prominent artists, athletes, and beautiful people. Its existence comes as a shock to our guide: by the moral standards he was reared on, and the expectations they fostered, the success of these people should have guaranteed their eventual failure:

> I attribute my pessimism to the fact that I was brought up in Los Angeles, where the fleeting brilliance of a career as an entertainer leaves a vast number of middle-aged, and even younger, casualties changing the sheets in motels and pumping gas. "Haven't I seen you before?" you ask the man who wipes your windshield in the car wash, and it turns out that he used to do a number called "Three Blind Mice" on national television when he was five years old. (41)

Los Angeles and Boston stand poles apart culturally, yet it takes little imagination to see a transplanted Puritan conscience at work here. The storyteller's earlier ethical frame of reference mandated severe retribution (in this life, admittedly) for earthly vanity, and thus he is stunned to find himself face to face with vanity carrying on much as it had before; a shade more subdued perhaps, but blessedly content nonetheless. Sinners (one thinks of the Saratoga racetrack crowd Cheever wrote about as a novice) as well as morally neutral superstars are happy beyond belief here, and will be forever:

> Here, throwing around a softball, were three .400 hitters, joking with Harry Newman, who pitched that shutout on a rainy, windy afternoon in St. Louis which led the team on to win their first pennant. . . . Here were yesterday's beauties, whom, had you been brought up in Los Angeles, you would have imagined to be pursuing their vanished splendor, stoned on alcohol or crucified on drugs.

There were even some great prostitutes here, a little heavy and un-
fresh, but still full of fun (41).

This is an updated Elysium, then, for those modern Prometheans
who dared to steal some of the divine fire in their heydays. Nothing of
great moment happens on the island—the accomplishments of its inhabitants are all in the past. The point, as Cheever develops it, is that
there need not be a settling of accounts between these souls and their
maker, during or after their lives. As with Shakespeare's Prospero, the
storytelling magician has actually *become* that maker. Near the end of a
lifetime that had experienced sin and degradation as intimately as it
knew exaltation and success, John Cheever indulged himself in a final,
whimsical act of hubris: his last experiment. A cynic once remarked
that as we grow older, we become more tolerant of others—simply because we have so much to tolerate in ourselves. On his imaginary island, John Cheever was finally able to come to terms with his own
success.

Conclusion

Literary historians of the future, if they avoid the passion for pigeon-holing, will find it difficult to assess John Cheever's place in twentieth-century American fiction. They will note that he had solid roots, personal and literary, in old New England, and that these nourished his storytelling ability, providing him with a cultural tradition, a "frame" for the larger story of his life's work. They will record that he was a prolific short story writer for the leading magazines of his time and came to be identified with a particular kind of narrative, set in the suburbs and combining serious themes with light poetic and occasionally fantastic effects. That is certainly the prevailing view at present, but as we have seen it is only partly correct. John Cheever defied categories while he lived, and so should his reputation.

Literary history offers numerous examples of writers who polished their skills to near-perfection, then exercised those abilities in a narrow channel for the rest of their careers. O. Henry took sentiment and the surprise ending as far as one could wish, and further. Sir Arthur Conan Doyle blended deft characterization and intellectual gamesmanship into a classic formula for the detective story. Artistically, the results in both cases, for mature readers, are identical: entertaining but very predictable stories.

John Cheever also sought to entertain his readers. His one inflexible rule, as a writer and teacher, was that a story must be interesting. His love of surprise *beginnings* demonstrates his awareness that busy, easily distracted readers must often be pulled into the miniature world of the short story. But it is what Cheever did with the imaginary—yet very real—inhabitants of his fictional worlds that sets him apart from more predictable writers. From one Cheever story to the next, the reader who follows his growth and development as a literary artist cannot sense in advance what his men and women will have to face, or how they will act. He was not as consistently excellent a maker of psychologically profound stories as William Faulkner or Ernest Hemingway, but he cannot be accused of resting content with storytelling approaches he had mastered. Over a long and productive career, he not only enlarged his narrative range by writing ambitious novels, but he also—and I believe more significantly—decided to extend his artistic reach in short fiction, by experimenting with technique and subject matter. In effect he refused to "play it safe" as an established writer in a certain mold, and after World War II charted a new, less certain course for his future. In so doing he made it possible for himself to succeed in ways that he had not ventured on earlier, and also to fail more ostentatiously. Through the next three decades he would do both, but ironically he succeeded so well that for most readers, his writing career would seem to have started in 1947.

I have tried to show that this is not the case. Cheever's decision, expressed in 1978, to consign his earlier work (almost half of his published short stories) to oblivion was apparently as deliberate as his earlier decision to break out of the naturalist mold and into a realm of fiction that he would have to create for himself. Yet I am convinced that this self-deprecation did both Cheever and his readers a serious disservice, by keeping several very good stories—among them "In Passing," "Frère Jacques," and "Manila"—in bound volumes on library shelves, and by preventing students from understanding how a writer like Cheever can progress from technical proficiency to classic status. At present there is reason to hope that this error, like Franz Kafka's command to burn his manuscripts, will be corrected, and that most of the better stories from the thirties and early forties will become more available to students and the reading public. If and when that occurs, these people—the thoughtful audience that Cheever increasingly cherished as he grew older—will surely discover the full range of his storytelling ability, and his reputation as one of America's best storytellers can only grow as a result.

I would also suggest that except for *The Wapshot Chronicle* and perhaps *Falconer*, Cheever's time and energy-consuming attempts to become an established novelist, as sensible as they were, only served to detract from his true vocation as a short story writer. A more serious mistake, of course, was the protracted and much-publicized drowning of his talent in alcohol; it is possible that the two mistakes are closely related, and together help to account for the acidic tone in much of his work.

On the other hand, critics have rightly faulted Cheever for failing to shake us out of our complacency when that was called for. "The Housebreaker of Shady Hill" is only one of many tales produced by this defiantly optimistic Cheever. And there were other literary sins as well. His insistence on working changes in his material and methods sometimes produced baffling results, as in "Christmas Is a Sad Season for the Poor" and "An Educated American Woman." Like other masters of the short story, Cheever was not immune from the weaknesses of facile caricature, tonal inconsistency, and outright propagandizing for pet ideas.

But success can only be measured against failure, and it can be argued that Cheever's failures paved the way for stories like "The Enormous Radio," "Goodbye, My Brother," "The Country Husband," and "The Swimmer"—stories in which just enough is said, and enough withheld, for the reader to catch a glimpse of the mysterious something that makes us human. For all his shortcomings, John Cheever knew that something well. To his great credit, to the very end he remained obsessed with the ethical conduct that gives life shape and meaning, and the record of his moral soundings is to be found in all of his published work.

"An Educated American Woman" is one of a handful of tales that show how narrow Cheever could be in his moral and sexual prejudices. But in several of the other stories I have discussed—stories like "The Season of Divorce" and "The Trouble of Marcie Flint"—he strikes off the chains of a spiteful morality and enlarges the range of his sympathies. And in so many others—among them "The Enormous Radio," "The Country Husband," and "The World of Apples"—he demonstrates that we are perfectly capable of punishing ourselves more effectively than any vengeful god could.

We are free to accept or reject the moral assumptions on which the stories rest, as well as their resolutions; that is an inescapable responsibility of our role as readers, and one that Cheever would have urged us to take. Although he never used his stories to preach, in almost everything he wrote from 1942 onward one can hear the voice of a prophet urging us to be kinder to each other. That particular eloquence, I believe, more than the brilliant sheen of his prose, was his true genius.

Notes

1. *New Republic* 64 (1 October 1930):171.
2. Annette Grant, "The Art of Fiction LXII: John Cheever," *Paris Review* 67 (Fall 1976):51.
3. *Atlantic Monthly* 157 (March 1936):331–43.

Notes

4. "Cheever Country," *New York Times Book Review*, 7 March 1982, 25.

5. I am grateful to Professor James McConkey, organizer of the conference, for this information.

6. "The Melancholy of Distance," in *Chekhov and Our Age*, ed. James McConkey (Cornell, N.Y.: Center for International Studies and Council of the Creative and Performing Arts, Cornell University, 1984), 134–35.

7. *Atlantic Monthly* 161 (March 1938):380.

8. *New Yorker* 18 (18 April 1942):14–16.

9. *New Yorker* 19 (7 August 1943):17–21.

10. I wish to thank Cheever's son Ben for permitting me to read, copy, and refer to his father's wartime correspondence with Mary Cheever.

11. From a personal interview with E. J. Kahn, Jr., Cheever's friend and colleague at the *New Yorker*.

12. *New Yorker* 21 (28 July 1945):20–23.

13. A notable counterexample would be "A Present for Louisa," published in *Mademoiselle*, December 1940, 126–27, 154–58; here Cheever does a surprising about-face from his objective stance, in the manner of O. Henry. A pair of young lovers finds true happiness in the face of economic hardship, straining credibility and pushing sentiment beyond the breaking point. The story almost seems to parody romantic fiction.

14. John Weaver was one of Cheever's Signal Corps colleagues, and their friendship continued until Cheever's death. In a series of letters and telephone interviews (1985–86), Mr. Weaver generously supplied me with as much helpful information about Cheever's wartime and postwar experiences as I could have wished for.

15. *SJC*, 33–41.

16. *New Yorker* 23 (16 August 1947):29–31.

17. See Susan Cheever's *Home Before Dark* (Boston: Houghton Mifflin, 1984), especially chapter 16.

18. *SJC*, 89–102.

19. Between 1931 and 1939 Cheever wrote five book reviews for the *New Republic*. For a complete listing see Dennis Coates's "John Cheever: A Checklist, 1930–1978" in *Bulletin of Bibliography* 36 (January–March 1979):1–13, 49.

20. *SJC*, 137–146.

21. Cheever often objected, unconvincingly, to analysis of his work as "crypto-autobiography"; see, for example, his interview with John Hersey, "John Cheever, Boy and Man," *New York Times Book Review*, 26 March 1978, 3 (included in this volume), and Wilfred Sheed, "Mr. Saturday, Mr. Monday and Mr. Cheever," *Life*, 18 April 1969, 44, 46.

22. *SJC*, 3–21.

23. Hersey interview, 3, 4.

24. In *Understanding Fiction*, 2d ed., ed. Cleanth Brooks and Robert Penn Warren (New York: Appleton-Century-Crofts, 1959), 571.

25. See Sheed's *Life* interview, 44, and Hersey's interview, 31.
26. *SJC*, 210–18.
27. *New Yorker* 30 (3 July 1954):18–23.
28. Dated 15 July 1962 and quoted in Bracher's incisive study of the *Chronicle*, "John Cheever and Comedy," *Critique* 6 (Spring 1963):72.
29. *The Wapshot Chronicle* (New York: Harper & Row, 1957), 21; the subsequent page reference, concerning Honora's will, is to this edition.
30. This is never mentioned in the *Chronicle*. It is brought out, almost anticlimactically, in *The Wapshot Scandal*.
31. "Facts of Living," *Saturday Review* 5 (30 September 1978):44.
32. *SJC*, 325–46.
33. *SJC*, 253–269.
34. "John Cheever and the Soft Sell of Disaster," in *Time to Murder and Create* (New York: David McKay, 1966), 175–76.
35. "The Domesticated Stroke of John Cheever," in *Critical Essays on John Cheever*, ed. R. G. Collins (Boston: G. K. Hall, 1982), 131.
36. *SJC*, 289–301.
37. Ibid., 404–412.
38. "Cheever and Hawthorne: The American Romancer's Art," in *Critical Essays on John Cheever*, ed. R. G. Collins (Boston: G. K. Hall, 1982), 197.
39. Cheever's tempered admiration for suburban folkways and mores is evident in an essay published in 1979, "Fiction Is Our Most Intimate Means of Communication," *U.S. News and World Report* 86 (21 May 1979):92.
40. Susan Cheever Cowley, "A Duet of Cheevers," *Newsweek*, 14 March 1977, 68.
41. Robert Gutwillig, "Dim Views through Fog," *New York Times Book Review*, 13 November 1960, 68.
42. *SJC*, 467–472.
43. "O'Hara, Cheever and Updike," *New York Review of Books*, 19 April 1973, 17.
44. *SJC*, 473–481.
45. Ibid., 498–511.
46. "John Cheever: The Art of Fiction LXII," *Paris Review* 17 (Fall 1976):57.
47. *SJC*, 521–535.
48. Ibid., 603–612.
49. "Cheever's Letters," *Vanity Fair* 47 (May 1984):63.
50. Scott Donaldson, *John Cheever* (New York: Random House, 1988), 208. I have used Donaldson's book to check biographical facts in this section and throughout my analysis, but I am responsible for any factual errors.

51. "A Grand Gatherum of Some Irate 20th-Century Weirdos," *New York Times Book Review* (27 April 1969), 1, 40.

52. *SJC*, 613–23.

53. Hersey (note 22), 32.

54. Donaldson 106 (note 50), 213–17.

55. *SJC*, 681–93.

56. Donaldson 108 (note 50), 268.

57. *Atlantic Monthly* 237 (April 1976), 43–45.

58. Walter Clemons, "Cheever's Triumph," *Newsweek* (14 March 1977), 61–62, 64, 67.

59. *New Yorker* 57 (27 April 1981), 41.

Part 2

THE WRITER

Introduction

A complete collection of Cheever's interviews, essays, and published statements on his own work and that of other writers would make a hefty volume. It would also be heavily weighted toward the last five years of Cheever's life, when he was much in demand for interviews and appearances because of the success of his novel *Falconer.* I have tried to include a chronologically representative selection of his views on life and literature, starting with a series of letters to his friend and mentor Elizabeth Ames and continuing with some astonishingly prescient comments printed in his hometown newspaper just as he was beginning to emerge from his apprenticeship as a writer. The short essay titled "What Happened" recounts the transformation from notes to story of "Goodbye, My Brother" and is thus the best record we have of Cheever's creative "method." In this light it might be usefully compared to my discussion of his World War II story "The Invisible Ship," which began as a series of letters to Mary Cheever.

Marcia Seligson's interview illuminates Cheever's literary background and tastes, shedding considerable light on his poetic interests. Students interested in tracing influences on his work may be pleasantly surprised by the catholicity of his reading. John Hersey's 1978 interview conveys all the mature wisdom one might expect from a conversation between two accomplished masters, and none of the self-importance; Cheever's views on New England's Puritan heritage and its effects on him are here forthrightly expressed.

Cheever's Letters

In 1933, in the depths of the Depression, a penniless but hopeful young man named John Cheever wrote to Elizabeth Ames, the formidable director of Yaddo, asking for admission to the famous artists' colony. Thus began an engaging correspondence that continued long after Cheever won renown as one of America's finest short-story writers and novelists. Here is a selection from Cheever's letters, which, from the very first, reveal his distinctive and ebullient voice.

Boston [1934]

Dear Mrs. Ames,

Last year at about this same time I wrote you, at Malcolm Cowley's suggestion, asking about coming to Yaddo. The letter was pretty late in the season and there was no room, and Mr. Cowley suggested that I write again this year.

He wrote you, I think, about my work. What or how much he said I don't know. The facts in the case are simple enough. I am twenty-two years old and have been writing for a number of years although I haven't published anything since 1932. I can vouch for the quantity if not for the quality and promise of the work I would do if there were a vacancy at Yaddo.

Everyone is, I imagine, reluctant to refer to the work in hand. I have lived all of my life within view of, and nearly every day of the last two years within, Boston. The city is old, out of step with the century, but age only seems to have quickened its elements. The Communists are clubbed in front of a staid, Georgian facade. Relics from the past continually pierce the present. Some dream of love survives the sandstone apartment houses. A paranoid ruins the Public Library. And within a half an hour's ride is the New England country where occasionally an abandoned house or a view surviving the hoardings and the hot-dog stands gives the memory an unexpected twist. The work in hand I think would deal with the horror and glory of this particular brick horizon.

The idea of leaving the city for a short while, after two uninterrupted years, has never been so distant or so desirable.

Sincerely yours,
John Cheever

East Weymouth, Massachusetts [1934]

Dear Mrs. Ames,

This is a late letter and it seems a long time since Lebanon Mountain came between us. Much longer than three weeks. Since then I've been living with my brother and his wife, trying to finish up some things that were started at Yaddo. I've been putting off the bus-ride to New York day after day until it can't be put off any longer. And so tonight I'll be rattling through Worcester, Hartford, etc.

A couple of editors are holding stories and there seems to be a chance of selling something soon. If I can get one printed I feel confident that the others will loosen up and the confidence and the money will be handy. It's been so long since I've printed anything and my work, through rejection, has grown so special that a consideration for readers will be a fine thing, I think.

Where I will be living and what I will do in New York is still up in the air but as soon as I find an address I'll write and if you should be in the city it would be fine to see you again.

As ever,
John Cheever

633 Hudson Street
New York City
[1934]

Dear Mrs. Ames,

Hudson Street is a far cry from anything in Boston and so far the difference stands in favor of Hudson Street. I arrived here on Wednesday and found some work at once. The income is still pretty precarious, the landlady worries and worries but I think it will hold out for another couple of weeks at least. I'm reading novels for M-G-M and some book reviewing may turn up next week. The income is barely enough to live on but enough if you go carefully. My only objection is that staying here and doing this work precludes all chances of doing work of my own. The work in itself doesn't take a great deal of time but during the hot weather Mrs. Lewton, the woman who rations out the work, keeps irregular and unpredictable hours and you spend more time waiting around for books and worrying about the next day's finances than you do in actual work. So it goes.

Giving up my own work, even temporarily, makes me impatient and discouraged. I still have the bundle of stories from Yaddo that are not completed and I would like to try a novel. I get tired of my own ways, tired of refinement, discretion, excessive detail, lack of action. Even while working there is a certain amount of impatience and when the work is suspended altogether the impatience increases. And it is almost impossible, after working over other people's books all day in this small room, to start up after supper and write a book of your own. If there should be a vacancy in Yaddo during September or October I would deeply appreciate it. . . .

And hoping to see you soon.

As ever,
John Cheever

23 Bethune Street, N.Y.C.
[1934]

Dear Mrs. Ames,

. . . So far it's been a lean strange winter. I have been able to make an irregular living off Metro-Goldwyn-Mayer. When they fail a check from some unexpected source usually falls like manna. The *New Republic* has taken a story and *Story* magazine is printing one in April. They have been recently printing dubious stuff but I'm satisfied with the story and that's what counts I guess. Also Harrison Smith shows signs of giving out an advance for a novel, something that I'm anxious to write.

. . . If you would like to read the story in *Story* I'll send up a copy. And if you are in New York and have the time, be sure and look me up.

As ever,
John Cheever

c/o Walker Evans
20 Bethune Street, New York City
[1934]

Dear Mrs. Ames,

. . . Two days in Boston were two days too many. It was pretty and the weather was clear and the crowds around Dock Square and Faneuil Hall were allright but the minute you go towards Pemberton Square and the Barrister's offices and Ashburton Place you begin to run into those pale, contrite faces. . . .

For the last couple of weeks I've been working as a photographer's assistant. And the *New Republic* and *Story* both took other stories so that was a little money. And I may be able to get a department store job for Christmas.

And if you are in the city be sure, if you have the time, to get in touch with me and we can have dinner together or something.

And as ever,
John Cheever

East Weymouth, Massachusetts
April 22, 1935

Dear Mrs. Ames,

. . . The winter hasn't exactly held any conquests, any literary conquests any rate. I've sold stories to the *New Republic* and the *New Yorker. Story* magazine has evidently decided to postpone the publication of my thing indefinitely. They are losing money and anxious to get newsstand circulation and the title ("Homage to Shakespeare") won't tempt anyone taking a train to Baltimore to buy a copy. I get worried sometimes about my inability to sell. It's about time I did. I got an agent a few days ago and this may help but I think the fault so far is mostly my own. When an editor hits an extraordinary story they know it and so far my stories haven't been good enough to jolt them. And in the meantime I've started a book which, I'm confident, will be very good. I've kept off a sustained thing for a long time, feeling that the novel (and its only definition seems to be negative) was created largely by and for the growth and decline of a middle-class that men of my generation are strangers to. Our lives have not been sustained or constant or ordered. Our characters don't die in bed. The powerful sense of

passed and passing time that seems to be the one definable and commendable quality of the novel is not our property. Our lives are not
long and well-told stories. But then these are not limitations. They
seem, in the course of work, to be exciting discoveries.

. . . I'm still anxious to hear from you about Yaddo or Triuna. There
seems to be a lot to do, everything to do in my case, and I would be
very grateful for a chance to write during the summer and I know that
there is no better place. If it would make it more possible I would be
glad to work for the chance. I can drive, swim well enough to be en-
trusted with a boat, handle an axe; nothing spectacular but generally
useful. And a job could probably be fitted in with working hours.

. . . I hope this finds you well and that you enjoyed your vacation
and the holiday. It was quite an event down here. It didn't rain. The
man in the next place stood out in the fields, looking up at the sun,
saying: "Where have I seen that before?" And I hope to see you soon.

As ever,
John Cheever

P.S. Remembering your interest in "miracles" I noticed in the local
evening paper that a silver crown, "Property of the Holy Ghost Society
Inc., of Bridgewater, Mass." has been credited with four small cures.
The crown, which is placed in the custody of the Society's President
during his term of office, is loaned for the use of anyone "who gives a
qualified reason for wanting it."

J.C.

Assinippi, Massachusetts
May 4, 1935

Dear Mrs. Ames,

. . . I was very glad to hear your advice about putting in time at some
other occupation besides writing. I have thought about it a lot and
worried about it a lot. And also your remarks about the expenditure of
energy in protection instead of adjustment. I can't help but view the
thing in an intensely personal light. I have thought about it continually
during the past winter and during the time I have been in Massachusetts. The problem is not, I think, the evasion of occupation and adjustment but the inability to find occupation and the enforced lack of

adjustment. It is not a problem peculiar to writers but the problem of an entire generation of younger men.

From the time when I took a job as a stock-boy in an abandoned subway tube when I was about fifteen, I have almost always worked. I have held the average run of jobs, driving a truck, working on a small newspaper etc. But about two years ago the possibility of holding these jobs stopped. I have no trade, no degree, no special training. Straightforward application for any kind of work from a bus-boy to an advertising copy-writer has been completely ineffectual. During the winter of '33 I held a part time job. In the winter of '34 I held a political job. I have supported myself this winter by writing synopses for M-G-M, not because I like to but because I can't find work as a loom-fixer or anything else. By pulling every possible wire I may be able to get a job in a ship-building plant this fall. I would much prefer it to any other opening; an editorial position.

The matter of adjustment seems to be a matter of personal courage and talent. Some people can have a great many lovers and take airplanes and trains from state to state and country to country and still remain cowards and children. Other people remain in one town and remain faithful to one wife and grow into mature and convincing men. There is a small number of scholars and artists who, through the illusion of research and work, fail to make any but the earliest adjustments and who you find at the ages of thirty and forty, sitting in the same rooms, weighing the same, unimportant decisions with their correspondence unmailed and the dust settling on their youths. But financial and emotional independence seems to make such a condition impossible. When you have no money you live, at least, in continual anxiety.

I've gone into this at length, I'm afraid, more to ease my own conscience than anything else, and I hope it hasn't been too confusing or dull. I hope to hear from you soon.

As ever,
John Cheever

Washington, D.C. [1936]

Dear Elizabeth,

. . . Things so far have been faster and more crowded than I imagine they will be when I get settled. I'm doing what is known as editorial work now. I hope to be able to transfer in a couple of weeks to something more interesting. . . .

You probably know Washington better than I and there's not much I can say about its physical appearance. I really know the inside of its trolley cars better than I do the character of its boulevards. The boarding house we live in is a little alcoholic as boarding houses go and for table mates we have two secretaries from the Russian embassy, two librarians, a man from the tariff commission, a government clerk and another man from my office. There is also an old old lady who sits at the head of the table and says all W.P.A. workers are lazy and good-for-nothing and she's finding it harder and harder to get me to pass her the lima beans.

One of the distinguishing features of this city is the rapid passage and the singular nature of its gossip. . . . In one evening you can pick up the news that . . . the commercial secretary of the Cuban embassy has been given a mysterious dismissal . . . [that] His Majesty's Government has asked His Majesty's Ambassador to drive around in an automobile less conspicuous than his Cord, and that Count P—pays the Italian embassy for the pleasure of sitting at a desk four hours a day, cutting pictures out of the newspaper, etc. A few days ago the widow of a General of the Regular Army took me into a corner and gave me a sure-fire solution for my success in Washington. "Now John L. Lewis has a daughter," she said. "She's rather stout and she's not awfully pretty but if you rush her, you're made."

I neglected to send you any money on my debt last pay day because of another increase in my obligations. I'm buying my father a set of teeth. That inexhaustible man went swimming a month ago. A wave picked him up, knocked him down, lifted out his teeth and swept them off into the bowels of the Atlantic.

Love,
John

Yaddo
February 1, 1937

Dear Elizabeth,

. . . My editors finally came through with a small sum of money and I returned to work on Thursday. Returning was very pleasant. There's nothing I'd rather do than work on the book. And no place where I'd rather work. The air is fine. The grounds are quiet. A man couldn't ask for more.

Before returning I went over to New York for a week and saw a few people I've been wanting to see. . . . It was exciting to be back there for a few days and I stared like a yokel at a couple in the Lafayette, drinking champagne and playing back-gammon. Then my brother appeared in town on Friday morning and I took the four o'clock train to Boston with him. It was a crowded week and I came up the Main Street of Quincy Friday night, while the iron bell in the church where John and John Quincy and Henry Adams worshipped was ringing nine.

New England was quite an experience. I haven't been home for as long in some years. . . . My father's memory is very acute and colorful and his story is exciting. He remembers the typhoid after the Civil War that laid an already impoverished and disillusioned Newburyport even lower. He remembers his mother's delirium and his Aunt Juliana who used to sit among the mandarin coats and ivory junks that her husband brought back from the east, and talk with an Indian "medium." His uncle Ebenezer was an abolitionist. He ran a biscuit factory that turned out hard-tack for the sailing vessels. When the war between the states was declared he was offered a contract by the government to make hard-tack for the soldiers. He rejected the offer because he felt that his hard-tack wasn't good enough for the Union soldiers. A competitor named Pierce then accepted the contract and made a fortune and founded a dynasty on the proceeds. Uncle Ebenezer had no regrets. He played the flute. The Pierce bakery has since grown into the National Biscuit Company while the wind whistles through Uncle Ebenezer's abandoned flour mill.

And then my father came up to Boston. . . . At the turn of the century he was shooting off Roman candles on the Common with the rest of his generation. He was making a lot of money then. Then come the stories of oyster sweep-stakes in Chesapeake Bay, storms on Lake Erie, express trains to Idaho, gold-rushes, horse-races, chaffard [*sic*] à la presse and mushrooms under glass, breakfasts in New Orleans, champagne, Shakespeare, boxing-matches, old age and failure. New England began its tragic decline. They tore down the Parker House. They closed the mills. And I saw Amoskeag last fall, looking at its own reflection in the Merrimack.

My brother is more interested in the situation than I am, I guess. . . . What concerns us both is some statement that the tradition

101

The Writer

is vigorous as well as reserved. Something that will disabuse the world
of the idea that all New England attics are full of crazy old aunts.

It's snowing now and it looks as though there might [be] some skiing tomorrow. . . .

As ever,
John

Quincy, Massachusetts
December 26, 1939

Dear Elizabeth,

Here I am again in what grandmother used to call the house of
plenty, sniffing the conflicting aromas of roast duck, Yardley's bath soap
and the fir balsam pillows maiden ladies distribute at Christmas. All in
all it's been a rousing holiday. A class-mate of mine had a party on
Christmas eve and we sat around a kitchen in Norwell and drank egg-
nog out of tennis trophies until two. Many of the kids I had been to
Thayer with were there, wearing eye-glasses and escorting pregnant
wives. Then back here, horse-back riding monday morning in the blue
hills, dinner with mother and dad and in the late afternoon we went
down to Norwell again and collected a lot of plaid socks, spotted ties,
and bright yellow gloves. The house was full of people, there was a lot
of champagne, three small children kept circling the living room,
breaking the springs in mechanical toys and hollering at the top of their
lungs, and a cable came from blacked-out Southampton announcing
that auntie Dess (one of the South African aunts) had arrived safely on
the blacked-out Scythia. The children played store, played house,
played tea-party, the women played bridge, the men played darts,
everyone stood knee deep in wrapping paper and outside the windows
you could see a light in the sky that is unlike anything I've ever seen
at the foot of New York's crosstown streets. The local squire showed
up with a jar of aspic, the children began to destroy the tree ornaments,
and driving home the moon was as bright as day and people were skating on every pond. So we remember the Prince of Peace, may it please
Him.

. . . The fact that I've been able to do more work in my three days
down here than I did in three weeks in New York is a proof I guess of

how quickly I respond to rural, or at least semi-rural surroundings and I don't look forward to returning to the musty interiors of the Hotel Chelsea. . . . The work I did in the city is no good, the amount of money I spent was crazy, and I haven't even got any memories. There's a lot to be learned by me about living.

Thanks a great deal for your Christmas card. It was the most modest and appropriate reminder I've seen. The significance, even the ironical significance, of Christmas seems to have been forgotten for the red light in the window and the public address system in the department store caroling Peace on Earth Goodwill to Men.

Love,
John

Quincy Youth Is Achieving New York Literary Career

*Mabelle Fullerton**

Quincy folk will do well to watch John Cheever, son of Mr. and Mrs. Frederick J. Cheever of 67 Spear Street, Quincy, who, without fanfare, is quietly but persistently achieving a literary career in New York.

An author of exceptional modesty, he says, "I really haven't written anything worth reading, yet." All this is in the face of publications in the *New Yorker*, the *Atlantic Monthly, Harper's Bazaar* and *Collier's*. Several of his short stories have also appeared in annual prize collections.

Now visiting at his home in Quincy, he will return to New York this week where he is currently at work on a contemporary novel with a New England background about Boston. "Possibly it will be finished in the spring," he thinks.

After leaving Quincy, Mr. Cheever spent some time at Yaddo, an artists' colony outside of Saratoga Springs, N.Y., where he did much writing.

He says he writes "pure fiction," though when pressed, admits that some of the articles in the *New Yorker* were based on experiences at the dancing classes he attended in Wollaston.

As for the mechanics of the art, he considers, "you have to write in a natural style, though some magazines permit more license than others. The magazines with the huge circulations are run as big businesses and have definite editorial policies and one of them is not to offend their best advertisers. It is also important to consider both the mental and income level which the magazine reaches and govern yourself accordingly."

He thinks, "It takes years to get anywhere, but you can keep on polishing away until you have something. The last decade has been pretty bad, as no great writers have appeared. The war, with its constant change, is undoubtedly going to have a great effect on writers. Now they seem to be getting away from the proletarian novel and there's an indication they may even go in for fantasy."

*Reprinted by permission from the *Quincy [Mass.] Patriot-Ledger*, 6 August 1940, 1, 7.

He opines that young writers or any wishing to achieve professional status do well to seek the service of an agent.

His idea of excellent modern writing is Carson Smith McCuller's "The Heart Is a Lonely Hunter."

His own literary style is ample proof that he writes naturally. It is simple, direct, forceful and has a quiet but deep humor. Because he believes he hasn't written anything "yet" and because you realize that he won't be satisfied until he has, he may be regarded as one of the white hopes of American literature.

What Happened

John Cheever*

A few years ago I stayed with my family in a rented house on Martha's Vineyard until the second week in October. The Indian Summer was brilliant and still. We went unwillingly when the time came to go. We took the mid-morning boat to Wood's Hole and drove from a brilliant day at the sea into humid and overcast weather. South of Hartford it began to rain. We reached the apartment house in the east Fifties where we then lived just before dark. The city in the rain seemed particularly cavernous and noisy and the summer was definitely ended. Early the next morning I went to the room where I work. Before leaving the Vineyard I had begun a story, based on some notes made a year or two earlier in New Hampshire. The story described a family in a summer house who spent their evenings playing backgammon. It probably would have been called "The Backgammon Game." I meant to use the checkers, the board and the forfeits of a game to show that the relationships within a family can be extortionate. I was not sure of the story's conclusion but at the back of my mind was the idea that someone would lose his life over the board. I saw a canoe accident on a mountain lake. Reading the story over that morning I saw that, like some kinds of wine, it had not traveled. It was bad.

I come from a Puritanical family and I had been taught as a child that a moral lies beneath all human conduct and that the moral is always detrimental to man. I count among my relations people who feel that there is some inexpugnable nastiness at the heart of life and that love, friendship, Bourbon whisky, lights of all kinds—are merely the crudest deceptions. My aim as a writer has been to record a moderation of these attitudes—an escape from them if this seemed necessary—and in the backgammon story I had plainly failed. It was in essence precisely the kind of idle pessimism that I had hoped to enlighten. It was in the vein of one of my elderly uncles who never put a worm on a fish hook without stating that sooner or later we will all be corruption.

*From *Understanding Fiction*, 2d ed., ed. Cleanth Brooks and Robert Penn Warren (New York: Appleton-Century-Crofts, 1959), 570–72. Reprinted by permission of Mary W. Cheever.

What Happened

In order to occupy myself more cheerfully I looked over the notes I had made during the summer. I first came on a long description of train-sheds and ferry-boat landings—a song to the engines of love and death—but the substance of this was that these journeys were of no import—they were a kind of deception. A few pages after this I came on the description of a friend who, having lost the charms of youth and unable to find any new lights to go by, had begun to dwell on his football triumphs. This was connected to a scathing description of the house in the Vineyard where we had spent a pleasant summer. The house had not been old, but it had been sheathed with old shingles and the new wood of the doors had been scored and stained. The rooms were lighted with electric candles and I linked this crude sense of the past to my friend's failure to mature. The failure, my notes said, was national. We had failed to mature as a people and had turned back to dwell on old football triumphs, raftered ceilings, candlelight and open fires. There were some tearful notes on the sea, washing away the embers of our picnic fires, on the east wind—the dark wind—on the promiscuity of a beautiful young woman I know, on the hardships of island farming, on the jet planes that bombed an island off Gay Head, and a morose description of a walk on South Beach. The only cheerful notes in all this were two sentences about the pleasure I had taken one afternoon in watching my wife and another young lady walk out of the sea without any clothes on.

It is brief, but most journeys leave us at least an illusion of improved perspective and there was a distance that morning between myself and my notes. I had spent the summer in excellent company and in a land-scape that I love, but there was no hint of this in the journal I had kept. The conflict in my feelings and my indignation at this division formed quickly in my mind the image of a despicable brother and I wrote: "Goodbye, My Brother." The story moved quickly. Lawrence arrived on the island on a voyage of no import. I made the narrator fatuous since there was some ambiguity in my indignation. Laud's Head had the accommodating power of an imaginary landscape where you can pick and choose from a wide range of memory, putting in the smell of roses from a very different place and the ringing of a tennis-court roller that you heard years ago. The plan of the house was clear to me at once, although it was unlike any house that I had even seen. The terrace, the living-room, the staircase all appeared in order and when I pushed open the door from the pantry into the kitchen I seemed to find there a cook who had worked for my mother-in-law the

107

year before the year before last. I had brought Lawrence home and taken him through his first night at Laud's Head before it was time for me to walk home for supper.

In the morning I unloaded onto Lawrence's shoulders my observations about backgammon. The story was moving then towards the boat club dance. Ten years ago at a costume ball in Minneapolis a man had worn a football uniform and his wife a wedding dress and this recollection fitted easily into place. The story was finished by Friday and I was happy for I know almost no pleasure greater than having a piece of fiction draw together incidents as disparate as a dance in Minneapolis and a backgammon game in the mountains so that they relate to one another and confirm that feeling that life itself is creative process, that one thing is put purposefully upon another, that what is lost in one encounter is replenished in the next and that we possess some power to make sense of what takes place.

On Saturday I took a train to Philadelphia with a friend to see a football game. The story was still on my mind but when I thought back over what I had written, looking for weakness or crudeness, I felt assured. The football game was dull. It got cold. I began to feel uneasy at the half. We left in the middle of the fourth quarter. I had not worn a top-coat and I was shivering. Waiting in the cold for the train back to New York I saw the true worthlessness of my story, the scope of my self-deceptions, the flights and crash-landings of an unstable disposition and when the train came into the station I thought vaguely of throwing myself onto the tracks; but I went instead to the club car and drank some whisky. I have read the story since, and while I see that Lawrence lacks dimension and that the ambiguity will estrange some readers, it remains a reasonably exact account of my feelings after returning to Manhattan after a long summer on Martha's Vineyard.

Portrait of a Man Reading

Marcia Seligson*

My earliest and clearest memories are of being read to at a very young age and constantly, by my mother and grandmother. In those days, and in my particular background—my mother was English and we lived right outside Boston in what I always think of as its "Athenian twilight years"—people read all the time, even people who were not terribly literate or erudite. They read alone, to each other, in groups, to their children. Reading was the commonest form of entertainment and family activity for us New England puritans.

What did your family read to you?

All of Dickens from beginning to end, read and re-read. As soon as I could, I tackled every one of these books myself. They also read me *Treasure Island* and *The Call of the Wild,* and some of the *Tom Swift* stories, which I finished for myself when I was able.

What else did you yourself read as a child?

I loved Poe but he was forbidden. I remember my friend's father had a set of Poe which he kept under lock and key. When he went out we'd force open the cabinet and read the stories to each other. When I was about ten I was taken to a performance of *The Merchant of Venice* in Boston. I went home and grabbed the complete Shakespeare off the shelf. But my family opposed my reading such heady stuff at my age and lured me back to Jack London. There was a lot of reading but a lot of restrictions, too.

What did you read in your teenage years?

It must sound awfully precocious but I started reading Proust at fourteen. I remember being absolutely enchanted with *Swann's Way,* appalled and shocked at *The Cities of the Plain.* I have re-read *Swann's Way,* but haven't picked up any other Proust since those years. I also read Joyce's *Ulysses* and all the Sherlock Holmes books when I was fifteen.

*Reprinted from the *Washington Post Book World,* 9 March 1969, 2, by permission of the publisher. ©1969 by the *Washington Post.*

The Writer

About that time I discovered John Donne and fell in love with poetry. I devoured Yeats, Eliot, the nineteenth-century Romantics, most of the Elizabethans.

Who were your favorites?
Yeats and Donne, I suppose. Donne's lines are so firm and solid, absolutely indestructible. Reading him involves a good bit of hard work, which I appreciate—being a New Englander.

Do you still read poetry?
A tremendous amount. I probably read as much poetry as fiction. Until recently, we had a very pleasant ritual in my family where everyone—my wife, our three children and I—gathered every Sunday afternoon at five o'clock in the living room, and each of us had to recite a poem he had learned and memorized during the week. When my youngest was seven, he was reciting Robert Frost. I had great fun learning Dylan Thomas's poetry, and many of the Psalms. One of the last things I memorized, before we discontinued the event, was Donne's "The Funeral."

Why are you so attracted to poetry?
It's one of the most acute means of communication we have for the things we feel deeply. It's odd—often at moments of stress, or during small, daily crises, I'll find the lines of a poem inadvertently running through my mind. I remember once missing a plane by minutes, standing at the gate watching it take off and feeling terribly frustrated and furious. Suddenly I realized the only thing circulating through my head was the line, "The force that through the green fuse drives the flower drives my green age," from Thomas's great poem.

What poetry have you read lately?
Donne and Yeats, of course. And I really like several of the younger poets writing now, like Alan Dugan, George Starbuck, John Ashbery and Ted Berrigan, for example.

What were you reading during the Thirties?
Hemingway, naturally, with great pleasure. Thomas Wolfe with less pleasure. I liked Faulkner. *The Sound and the Fury* and *As I Lay Dying* were favorites of mine. I was not politically obsessed, as so many of my writer friends were in those years. But I did get caught up in the

110

spirit of the times to the extent that I devoted myself to reading all of the Russians from Gogol on.

Do you read in any other languages?

Yes, French and Italian—both learned in prep school. I used to try to read one book a year in each, but now I've gotten horribly lazy. I must admit I haven't gotten through a novel in Italian in four or five years, although I did prefer reading in Italian to French.

What books have you read recently in French?

Madame Bovary, several times, and *The Fall* by Camus. I chose that particular one because it's his shortest novel.

How about reading short stories?

I've been especially interested in a few writers today who use the short story as a form of moral parable. Dino Buzzati, an excellent Italian writer and a devout Catholic, is one I admire a great deal. Also Marcel Aymé, who is an anticleric, and Flannery O'Connor—another Catholic. Their stories are based on strong moral positions, and tremendous discipline is needed to develop these premises well in the period of time a short story has allowed to it. John O'Hara, too, writes highly moral tales. Look how his wicked people are always burning in hell.

Do you read history, biography, science fiction, mysteries?

Sometimes I become very immersed in a specific period of history and will read everything I can find. Recently I read four books on the period from 1780 to 1812 in France. I've also done some reading on the Risorgimento and the two Garibaldi campaigns. I've read a pile of books on the Russian Revolution over the years, most of them quite bad. Occasionally I read biographies; this past year I found Michael Holroyd's biography of Lytton Strachey fascinating. I'm not at all interested in science fiction. And I haven't looked at a mystery novel since my entire family put down everything we were reading and for a solid week read nothing but James Bond books.

Do you go to the theater?

Almost never. I lead a very secluded, boozy life in the woods in upstate New York. If I'm not writing or reading, I skate, swim, visit, walk with my dogs, eat, drink. Occasionally we get to a film at the local movie theater, but mostly we all read. My wife is much more erudite than I, and our children love to read aloud. We have quite a large, serviceable library in our home, and all tend to have very catholic tastes. I often don't finish a book, may put it down after three sentences, but I'm always involved in reading *something*.

What have you read in the last year?

Let's see, I can hardly remember everything I've read—I have re-read Gibbon as well as several Dickens novels of which I'm still extremely fond. Many of my reading decisions are made for me by my family, since this is an activity we frequently do together. For instance, my son read Stephen Crane for the first time this year, so I re-read him. Also *My Antonia* by Willa Cather, a marvelous book. We all read George Eliot's *Middlemarch*. And the Nile books, by Alan Moorehead.

Do you keep up with current American fiction?

Certainly. I just finished *Portnoy's Complaint*—an absolutely glorious, important work.

Why do you feel Portnoy's Complaint *is such an important book?*

It's a most exceptional novel. The tone is always perfect, the control flawless. The book is wonderfully pure, considering his subject matter. The descriptions of fairly unsavory sexual encounters are beautifully, wittily done. And nobody has handled the subject of masturbation with any real candor until this book. Roth is masterful at pitching one mood against another—humor, pathos, self-satire. He always knows exactly what he's doing. I certainly think he's one of the best writers we have in America.

What other American writers are you interested in today?

I've always found Updike's career very exciting. He's an adventurer, a traveler. He never repeats himself and he takes all sorts of chances in the directions he's willing to go off into. For example, you know his early reputation was made as a humorous poet and his last novel swung out into a venereal obsession. We have no idea where he'll go next.

Anybody else?

I admire Mailer tremendously, especially *The Armies of the Night*. And Bill Styron, Robert Penn Warren, Saul Bellow is excellent—I think *Henderson the Rain King* is a brilliant book.

112

Portrait of a Man Reading

Could you choose a favorite of this group?

No, I really don't think of contemporary literature as a competitive sport. There is such a tremendous conflagration of work being done by so many writers, each attempting something different. In the same way, I'm not fond of categorization. I really don't care if a book is "journalistic fiction" or "fictional journalism" or "non-fiction fiction." Literature is a means of communication and that's all that is crucial. Also, I must admit that my own literary taste is quite impetuous and I find it difficult to diagnose such impulsive responses. I think very few writers, myself included, have trustworthy or responsible reading tastes.

Do you have a very favorite book?

Yes, definitely. *Madame Bovary.* I've probably read it twenty-five times, many of those in French.

Why is it such a great novel?

Because the writing is absolutely precise and simply perfect. This book was a considerable turning point in fiction, an innovation. Of course, all great novels are innovations but *Madame Bovary* was, for one thing, the first account we have of controlled schizophrenia. And it is a highly adventurous moral tale. You know the book was censored when it was first published and Flaubert was taken to court. Undoubtedly the most offensive point in the book is when Emma sits on a table and smokes a cigarette.

John Cheever, Boy and Man

*John Hersey**

March a year ago, on the occasion of the publication of John Cheever's "Falconer," the Book Review commissioned and ran an interview with Mr. Cheever by John Hersey, Yale Alumni Magazine and Journal, for its December 1977 issue specially devoted to the arts at Yale, asked Mr. Hersey to interview Mr. Cheever again. A major part of the interview follows. Mr. Hersey's most recent novel is "The Walnut Door."

Q: I'd like to talk first with you, John, about some of the things behind the work—matters of education, family, experience, and so on—that have given you the resources you've dealt with so well. You're one of the best educated men, to say nothing of writers, that I know. But you are a paradigm of the man of letters who is unspoiled by higher education. You raise the question in our minds whether writers should go to school at all. Your formal, or institutional, education was broken off when you were bounced from Thayer Academy at the age of 17. I wonder if you'd like to begin by telling us about that experience?

A: I was delighted to be expelled from Thayer. It was not unreasonable on their part. They would have liked very much for me to go on to Harvard, and I sensed intuitively that that would have been disastrous. So I was very happy when the headmaster threatened me with expulsion, and I immediately went home and wrote an article for The New Republic, called "Expelled," which The New Republic published. I was 17 when it was published, and I was very happy about it.

Q: What was the immediate cause of your expulsion?

A: Smoking, an expulsion offence.

Q: Who caught you? Were you caught with the crime blazing?

A: I was caught by a teacher.

Q: Was it exciting?

A: It was intentional, John.

*Reprinted from the *New York Times Book Review*, 26 March 1978, 3, 31–34, by permission of the publisher. © 1978 by the New York Times Company.

John Cheever, Boy and Man

Q: Let me read about a family from a Cheever story. "The branch of the Pommeroys to which we belong was founded by a minister who was eulogized by Cotton Mather for his untiring abjuration of the Devil. The Pommeroys were ministers until the middle of the 19th century, and the harshness of their thought—man is full of misery, and all earthly beauty is lustful and corrupt—has been preserved in books and sermons. The temper of our family changed somewhat and became more light-hearted, but when I was of school age, I can remember a cousinage of old men and women who seemed to hark back to the dark days of the ministry and to be animated by perpetual guilt and the deification of the scourge. If you are raised in this atmosphere—and in a sense we were—I think it's a trial of the spirit to reject its habits of guile, self-denial, taciturnity and penitence." Does this describe at all the family in which you grew up?

A: Yes, it does. Of course I am describing a character in fiction, and any confusion between autobiography and fiction is lamentable. The darkness—the capacity for darkness that was cherished by New England—certainly colored our lives. My father used to point to his veins and say, "There is nothing in these veins but the blood of shipsmasters and schoolteachers." As a matter of fact, he had a couple of old cousins who were obviously native Indians. I don't know how he included them. The Cheevers, I believe, did marry Indians.

Q: Could you talk about your childhood?

A: How truthfully or how persuasively, I don't know. I recall it as having been extremely sunny. This may be a reaction to the tradition of the novelist as being a man who had a wretched childhood, an even worse adolescence, and spent the rest of his life trying in some way to rectify these injuries—something one would not want to encourage. My recollections of childhood are of the Cape and of southern Massachusetts. All seemed quite pleasant. The traumatic years that I went into in psychoanalytical conversations dealt with my adolescence, and with the fact that my parents separated. My brother and I became very close—morbidly close, it seemed to me. It was a very intense relationship in traditional Boston which was, at that point, so anxious to fortify its own eccentricities that anything so peculiar as two brothers who were inseparable was greeted enthusiastically. It seemed to me that two men living with such intense intimacy was an ungainly arrangement, that there was some immutable shabbiness about any such life. He was a cotton textile manufacturer, and I was to be the novelist. At the age of 19 we traveled in Europe together and then I walked, so far as possible, out of his life.

Q: The brother figure in your work, certainly in "Falconer," is one who suffers at the hand of the narrator. And yet you were very close to this brother.

A: I don't suppose that I have ever known a love so broad as my love for my brother. I've known loves that are much more enduring, much richer, much more brilliant, much more rewarding. But this seems to have been a very basic love. The brother theme appears in a great many stories. I strike him in some, I hit him with sticks, rocks; he in turn also damages me with profligacy, drunkenness, indebtedness, and emotional damage. And in "Falconer," the brother is killed. There are, of course, historical precedents: Osiris and Set in Egypt; Cain and Abel; the Dioscuri in Rome. So that the brother theme, though it is not one of the dominating themes in literature, has some universality.

Q: A minute ago, you said, "I strike my brother." How close are you to your narrator?

A: It seems to me that any confusion between autobiography and fiction debases fiction. The role autobiography plays in fiction is precisely the role that reality plays in a dream. As you dream your ship, you perhaps know the boat, but you're going towards a coast that is quite strange; you're wearing strange clothes, the language that is being spoken around you is a language you don't understand, but the woman on your left is your wife. It seems to me that this not capricious but quite mysterious union of fact and imagination one also finds in fiction. My favorite definition of fiction is Cocteau's: "Literature is a force of memory that we have not yet understood." It seems that in a book that one finds gratifying, the writer is able to present the reader with a memory he has already possessed, but has not comprehended. Does that make sense?

Q: It does in terms of the relationships we've been talking about— father/son, brother/brother, and so on. The father/son theme occurs again and again very strongly in your work, and occasionally the mother appears in a vivid way. What about your own mother?

A: Here again, John, it was a relationship that I was able superficially to requite. I was correct. I visited both my parents four times a year until they died. My father asked that I read Prospero's speech over his grave, which I did. It was not requited in any way in the sense that my

116

John Cheever, Boy and Man

relationship, and my wife's relationship, is to our children. It was never intimate, but it seems not to have been destructive. The psychiatrist, of course, disagrees with me.

Q: What about some relationships with others whom you encountered in early years, who may have been proxies for parents or teachers?

A: The generosity I received—it seems to me that the generosity most people will receive as young men and women—is inestimable. Malcolm Cowley singled the article "Expelled" out of a pile of unsolicited manuscripts and sent me a telegram, which was exciting. And, at 65, I trust I can do something of that sort for the young.

Q: You encountered some older writers when you went to New York, did you not?

A: Yes, I think I was perhaps the only man in the northeast who talked with Sherwood Anderson. E. E. Cummings was a dear friend. I met him when I was 18, loved him immediately, and very much love his memory. Dos Passos I knew, and thought him rather dull, but pleasant. Edmund Wilson I met again and again, and we both detested one another. Cummings was very exciting and very helpful. I was in the army for four years, in an infantry company, and got a letter from him which included a $10 bill, an autumn leaf, and the line, "I too have slept with someone else's boot in the corner of my smile."

Q: You were living, certainly in no affluence, in New York in the 30's. Some of your acquaintances were very political people, and you had some experience of the Second World War. Yet one doesn't feel the wind, in your work, of the kinds of literary influences that politics brought to bear on much of writing in the 30's, and that the war brought on much subsequent writing.

A: On the political matter in the 30's, it seemed to me that the Communist Party attempted to take over, to direct, writing. This was very serious. People—Newton Arvin, for example, who was a friend and a very good critic—decided that the only literature was the literature that would provoke social change. This struck me as being rubbish. And then, when I was perhaps 20, I was singled out by Marxist critics in *New Masses* magazine as the final example of bourgeois degeneration. This more or less closed any political relationships with the Communist Party. On the war—I have written about it, but very little. My feeling was, when I found myself in the particular chaos of the infantry, that there must be deeper, richer strata to life. There are, of course.

117

The Writer

Q: And what about your life with Mary? Your family life?

A: I claim to have been married for 40 years. My wife claims, I think, 35. It's been an enormously rich, various experience. We've thought of divorcing once a month, at least, over these 40 years. Perhaps the most exciting thing in life for me has been the birth of my children. In interviews people always say, "Well, what was the most exciting thing in your life?" And I say, "The birth of my children." And they say, "Well then, after that?" The amount of richness that children bring into the lives of their parents is indescribable. I've never been rich. When I wanted to be a writer my parents said, "Well, you may be a writer"—this is again the voice of New England—"so long as you don't pursue fame or wealth." And I said, "Well, I have no idea of being famous or wealthy"—an idea I've often regretted.

Q: In "Goodbye, My Brother," the husband and wife go to a costume party at a club. She dresses as a bride, he as a football player. They discover, to their amusement at first, that there are a dozen women who come as brides, and enough football players to have a good scrimmage. Do you see nostalgia as a reaching back? As a wish for a past in exchange for a present that's less pleasant?

A: That would be, I think, much more regressive than nostalgia. Nostalgia is the longing for the world we all know, or seem to have known, the world we all love, and the people in it we love. Nostalgia is also a passion, a longing not only for that which is lost to us, or which has been destroyed or burned, or which we've outgrown; it is also a force of aspiration. It is finding ourselves not in the world we love, but knowing how deeply we love it, enjoying some conviction that we will return, or discover it, or discover the way to it.

Q: In a story about a well-digger named Artemis, you say his drill "struck the planet sixty blows a minute." And that trivial activity of trying to find water for one house begins to have music of stars in it because you've enlarged it by that one strange choice of the word "planet." There are other characters, though, who seem to make things smaller. "The seraphic look she assumed when she was listening to music was the look of someone trying to recall an old phone number."

A: I think one has a choice, with imagery, either to enlarge or to diminish. At this point I find diminishment despicable. When I was a younger man I thought it brilliant. But as a mature novelist I think one's responsibility is to perhaps get a few more details in and come out with a somewhat larger character. Chekhov, in his journals, urges the writer to know as much as he possibly can about a character—his shoe size, his liver condition, any tendency he might have to lordosis, his lungs, clothes, habits, intestinal tract—and then, from this glossary, to pick one detail. It is a judgment of character by a single attribute.

Q: On pleasure and pain. You once said to me that you had no memory of pain, but you have, at any rate, a clear memory of pleasure. You see your characters, time and again, responding almost ecstatically to things around them, even when the general situation of their lives may be quite terrible.

A: That has been my experience.

Q: These are memories?

A: In Bulgaria, where we were recently, someone said, "You are a naïve optimist." Of course, it's a very general term—one I would qualify—but I would be quite happy to be classified, in Bulgaria, as a naïve optimist.

Q: Finally, there is the tension between light and dark. The sky appears in almost every one of your stories, usually with a vivid sense of welcome. It's terribly important in "Falconer," that little patch of sky that's seen outside the prison windows.

A: Light is very important to me, very important to my moods. Blue sky. I always go back to William James, of course. A blue sky is quite mysterious, mysteriously heartening, a source of indescribable joy. Light and dark, very loosely of course, mean good and evil. And one is always seeking to find out how much courage, or how much intelligence, or how much comprehension, one can bring to the choice between good and evil in one's life.

Q: Could it be that the heart attacks you had some years ago, and your struggle with drinking and triumph over that in your life, were realized in the kind of leap that "Falconer" has achieved?

A: Obviously there's a connection. I resist admitting it because this puts the novel into an autobiographical context. I had started to write "Falconer" when I was in Boston, when I was drunk and drugged much of the time, putting hats on the statuary on Commonwealth Avenue, and so forth. However, I did not complete the novel until I had some rather grueling experiences in both alcohol and drug withdrawal, and I was delighted to be free. That, obviously, is part of the book.

The Writer

I'm very reluctant to admit it because I would not want the novel to be thought an account of Cheever's escape from a rehabilitation center. I wanted to write as dark and as radiant a book as possible. I didn't know that the hero would get out of prison until I was about halfway through. I came running out of the house and shouted, "He's going to get out. Hey! Hey! He's going to get out." I was probably convinced that he was going to escape before I started, but it was at some more obscure stratum of my intelligence. I wanted to write about confinement.

Part 3

THE CRITICS

Introduction

With a few exceptions, Cheever's work was not highly regarded by serious critics throughout most of his life. Like other writers stamped with the *New Yorker* seal of approval, he was damned by the success associated with consistent publication in that magazine: to be a *New Yorker* writer was to be safe, acceptable, and predictable—all evidence to the contrary notwithstanding. Nonetheless, some careful readers like Struthers Burt detected, early on, a "classic" quality of considerable promise in Cheever's apprentice work, the stories that Cheever himself would later find embarrassing for their roughness.

Alfred Kazin's indictment of Cheever's predictability, although not persuasive, is well-reasoned and evenhanded. But I have also included an excerpt from a Scott Donaldson essay surveying Cheever's career, primarily because it focuses so sharply on the issue of Cheever's unique identity as a short story writer, as opposed to his putative *New Yorker* identity.

Genuine, painstaking stylistic analysis is usually so formidable and thankless a task that only the bravest or most foolhardy of scholars will choose to attempt it. Cheever added a uniquely poetic flavor to the telling of his best stories; describing the operation of this music on our senses requires both insight and sensitivity. In their studies of Cheever's style, George Hunt and Robert Morace prove that such analysis need not be reductive. Their pioneering work should inspire those who feel that in the case of Cheever's unique alchemy, style often became substance.

John Cheever's Sense of Drama
*Struthers Burt**

Unless I am very much mistaken, when this war is over, John Cheever—he is now in the army—will become one of the most distinguished writers, not only as a short story writer but as a novelist. Indeed, if he wishes to perform that ancient triple-feat, not as popular now as it was twenty years ago in the time of Galsworthy and Bennett and their fellows, he can be a playwright too, for he has all the necessary signs and characteristics. The sense of drama in ordinary events and people; the underlying and universal importance of the outwardly unimportant; a deep feeling for the perversities and contradictions, the worth and unexpected dignity of life, its ironies, comedies, and tragedies. All of this explained in a style of his own, brief, apparently casual, but carefully selected; unaccented until the accent is needed. Meanwhile, he has published the best volume of short stories I have come across in a long while, and that is a much more important event in American writing than most people realize.

The short story is a curious and especial thing, a delicate and restricted medium in which many have walked, but few succeeded. It is like the sonnet in poetry; the only artificial (I mean in technique, not content) form of poetry that has ever been able to make itself thoroughly at home within the realms of that magnificent, impatient, sensible, and beautiful mode of human expression, the English language, and, like the sonnet, the short story has, or should have, the same limitations of space, of concentrated emotion, of characters, of theme and events. Never by any chance should it be the scenario, the skeleton, of something longer. Its strength, like the sonnet's, comes from deep emotion and perception, and, when necessary, passion, beating against the inescapable form that encircles it. As in the sonnet, as indeed in all good poetry, not a word or line, or figure of speech, or simile, must be amiss or superfluous. The author has just so many minutes in which to be of value, and the contest—the selection—in

*From the *Saturday Review* 26 (24 April 1943), 9. Copyright 1943 by the *Saturday Review*. Reprinted with permission.

his mind is between what he would like to say, and what he should say; the search is for the inevitable phrase and sentence and description that contain the final illumination but which, at the same time, seem inevitable and natural.

As a result, probably not more than a score of truly great short stories have ever been written. The same holds true of sonnets. Even the great masters of the short story, Chekhov, Turgeniev, Maupassant, Kipling, O. Henry in his better moments, and others, only reached their culmination in a few instances. The short story, like electricity, gains its power through its amperage. It is a bullet whose penetration is due to a force poured through a narrow channel. Of all forms of writing it is the most difficult.

The present volume consists of thirty short stories most of which have appeared in the *New Yorker*, the *Yale Review*, and *Story* magazine, and one can see the compression used, for the book is only two hundred and fifty-six pages long. Many of the stories are only a few pages in length, a thousand, twelve hundred words; and at least half of them are eminently successful; a quarter are far above the average; all are well done; and only a couple fail. "Of Love; A Testimony," except for its title, is one of the best love stories I have ever read. There is a curious and interesting development in the book, and in the procession of the stories—the way they are placed—that ties the volume together and gives it almost the feeling of a novel despite the inevitable lack of connection between any short stories. The earlier stories have to do with the troubled, frustrated, apparently futile years of 1939 and 1941; and then there are some beautifully told stories of the average American—the average American with a college degree, the same suburbanite—actually at war, but still in this country. This gives the book the interest and importance of a progress toward Fate; and so there's a classic feeling to it.

No one can tell how many artists, musicians, writers, painters, sculptors, are in our armed forces. They will not emerge for some years yet. When they do there should be something interesting, for these younger men have learned a lot, apparently, and apparently it's part of their make-up. They are just as honest and ruthless as their predecessors, perhaps even more so, but they have regained in some mysterious way their belief in irony and pity and the catharsis, which despite the Greeks, and Anatole France, the last who announced their necessity, have for some time been regarded as sentimental clichés.

John Cheever has only two things to fear; a hardening into an especial style that might become an affectation, and a deliberate casualness and simplicity that might become the same. Otherwise, the world is his.

O'Hara, Cheever and Updike
*Alfred Kazin**

John Cheever found in suburbsville almost as many cruel social differences as O'Hara had always known in Gibbsville. But the overwhelming sensation that a reader got from Cheever's special performance of the short story was of a form that no longer spoke for itself. It was not even a "slice of life," as O'Hara's stories were, but had become a demonstration of the amazing sadness, futility, and evanescence of life among the settled, moneyed, seemingly altogether domesticated people in Proxmire Manor. As Cheever said in two different pieces of fiction, Why, in this "half-finished civilization, in this most prosperous, equitable and accomplished world, should everyone seem so disappointed?" It is a question that earlier writers of "*The New Yorker* story" would not have asked openly, with so much expectation of being agreed with, and twice. But Cheever's brightly comic charming, heartbreaking performances always came out as direct points made about "the quality of life in the United States," or "How We Live Now."

Cheever—Salinger and Updike were to be like him in this respect—began and somehow has remained a startlingly precocious, provocatively "youthful" writer. But unlike Salinger and Updike, he was to seem more identifiable with the rest of *The New Yorker,* just as his complaint about American life was more concrete and his fiction more expectable. As I've written before, his stories regularly became a form of social lament-writing never hard to take. What they said, and Cheever openly *said* it, was that America was still a dream, a fantasy; America did not look lived in. Americans were not really settled in. In their own minds they were still on their way to the Promised Land. In story after story Cheever's characters, guiltily, secretly disillusioned and disabused with their famous "way of life" (always something that could be put into words and therefore promised, advertised, and demonstrated), suddenly acted out their inner subversion. They became "ec-

*Reprinted with permission from the *New York Review of Books* (19 April 1973), 14–18. © 1973 Nyrev, Inc.

centrics," crazily swimming from pool to pool, good husbands who fell in love with the baby sitter. Sometimes, like "Aunt Justina," they even died in the living room and could not be moved because of the health laws and restriction by the zoning law on any funeral parlors in the neighborhood.

Acting out one's loneliness, one's death wish—any sudden eccentricity embarrassing everybody in the neighborhood—these make for situation comedy. Life is turning one's "normal" self inside out at a party. The subject of Cheever's stories is regularly a situation that betrays the basic "unreality" of some character's life. It is a trying-out of freedom in the shape of the extreme, the unmentionable. Crossing the social line is one aspect of comedy, and Cheever demonstrates it by giving a social shape to the most insubstantial and private longings. Loneliness is the dirty little secret, a personal drive so urgent and confusing that it comes out a vice. But the pathetic escapade never lasts very long. We are not at home here, says Cheever. But there is no other place for us to feel that we are not at home.

In these terms the short story becomes not the compression of an actual defeat but the anecdote of a temporary crisis. The crisis is the trying-out of sin, escape, the abyss, and is described by Cheever with radiant attention: *there* is the only new world his characters ever reach.

> . . . They flew into a white cloud of such density that it reflected the exhaust fires. The color of the cloud darkened to gray, and the plane began to rock. . . . The stewardess announced that they were going to make an emergency landing. All but the children saw in their minds the spreading wings of the Angel of Death. The pilot could be heard singing faintly, "I've got sixpence, jolly jolly sixpence. I've got sixpence to last me all my life. . . ."

The "country husband" in this most brilliant of Cheever's stories returns home to find that his brush with death is not of the slightest interest to his family, so he falls in love with the baby sitter. He does not get very far with the baby sitter, so he goes to a therapist who prescribes woodworking. The story ends derisively on the brainwashed husband who will no longer stray from home.

But who cares about this fellow? It is Cheever's clever, showy handling of the husband's "craziness," sentence by sentence, that engages us. Each sentence is a miniature of Cheever's narrative style, and each sentence makes the point that Cheever is mastering his material, and comes back to the mystery of why, in this half-finished civilization, this most prosperous, equitable, and accomplished world, everyone should seem so disappointed. So there is no mastery in Cheever's story except Cheever's. It is Cheever one watches in the story, Cheever who moves us, literally, by the shape of his effort in every line, by the significance he gives to every inflection, and finally by the cruel lucidity he brings to this most prosperous, equitable, and accomplished world as a breaking of the heart.

My deepest feeling about Cheever is that his marvelous brightness is an effort to cheer himself up. His is the only impressive energy in a perhaps too equitable and prosperous suburban world whose subject is internal depression, the Saturday night party, and the post-martini bitterness. Feeling alone is the air his characters breathe. Just as his characters have no feeling of achievement in their work, so they never collide with or have to fight a society which is actually America in allegory. All conflict is in the head. People just disappear, as from a party. Cheever's novels—*The Wapshot Chronicle, The Wapshot Scandal, Bullet Park*—tend to muffle his characters in meaning even more than the short stories do. Cheever is such an accomplished performer of the short story that the foreshortening of effect has become second nature with him. There is the shortest possible bridge between cause and effect. *The New Yorker* column is still the inch of ivory on which he writes. Cheever always writes about "America." He is an intellectual. The Wapshot novels are wholly allegories of place showing the degeneration of the old New England village, "St. Botolph's," into the symbolic (but spreading) suburb that is "Proxmire Manor. . . ."

John Cheever
Scott Donaldson*

Cheever's comedy is fully capable of making his readers laugh out loud. And it may be that to some extent Cheever's "marvelous brightness," as Alfred Kazin wrote, represents an effort to cheer himself up.

*An excerpt from the entry "John Cheever" in *American Writers: A Collection of Literary Biographies*, suppl. 1, part 1, ed. Leonard Ungar (New York: Charles Scribner's Sons, 1979), 195–97. Reprinted by permission of Charles Scribner's Sons, an imprint of Macmillan Publishing Co. © 1979 by Charles Scribner's Sons.

Certainly he derives affirmation from unprepossessing materials. But the author himself attributes his fictional attitude to another motive. "One has an impulse to bring glad tidings to someone. My sense of literature is a sense of giving, not a diminishment." He has aimed, in his writing, "to make some link between the light in the sky and the taste of death." Death will intrude, but light remains the goal. "Man's inclination toward light, toward brightness, is very nearly botanical— and I mean spiritual light. One not only needs it, one struggles for it." This set of mind suits ill with the lugubrious tone of much modernist writing, with what Gardner calls "the tiresome modern fashion of always viewing the universe with alarm, either groaning or cynically sneering."

Nor has Cheever's critical reputation benefited from the periodical company he has kept. Despite his novels, he is still regarded by many as the quintessential *New Yorker* story writer. The stories in that most successful of middle-class, middlebrow magazines are supposed to run to a pattern: they focus on a single incident, but in the telling suggest echoes from the past and omens for the future. The settings are regional, most often New York or its suburbs—"The Connecticut Story," William Van O'Connor called it. The hero—or rather protagonist, for there are no heroes in *New Yorker* stories—is characterized by his sensitivity; he is a man of feeling, not of action. Plot is unimportant; and readers sometimes complain that "nothing happens" in these stories. Certainly little happens at the end; and it is said that to get a *New Yorker* ending, one need only cut off the last paragraph of a more conventional one. The stories in the magazine may instruct, but they must entertain.

The *New Yorker* has served as patron to John Cheever for four decades, although he has rarely written "a *New Yorker* story"—elegant, charming, inconsequential—since his first book was published in 1943. In the later stories characters are fully fleshed out, plots are more complicated, violence smolders or erupts, and the setting shifts at times to overseas locations, particularly to Rome. Yet so pervasive is the power of the stereotype and so well known Cheever's connection with the magazine that as recently as 1973 Kazin remarked that "The *New Yorker* column is still the inch of ivory on which he writes."

Furthermore, Cheever suffered temporary critical ostracism when *Time* magazine, that still more pervasive voice of middle-class values, proclaimed his virtues in a March 1964 cover story. The story was headed "Ovid in Ossining," but it "offered Cheever to the world"—in

John W. Aldridge's phrase—"as a kind of crew-cut, Ivy League Faulkner of the New York exurbs, who could be both artistically sincere and piously right-thinking about the eternal verities": a Faulkner one could count on, for one knew the territory. What was good enough for *Time* tended to alienate critics such as the one who observed, accurately enough, that "if Cheever were Swift, *Time* would be more worried about him." By sticking to his desk (or rather a series of desks, for he habitually works on each new book in a different room of his house), Cheever has managed to write his way out of the ill effects of such middlebrow praise. He tries to avoid taking the issue of critical acceptance too seriously; he often arranges to be out of the country when a book is scheduled to appear. Only in the case of *Falconer* has he submitted to the invasion of the writer's privacy so hungrily sought by the practitioners of publicity.

In any case, he has earned his share of more meaningful recognition. *The Wapshot Chronicle* won the National Book Award for fiction in 1958. *The Wapshot Scandal* was awarded in 1965 the still more prestigious Howells medal of the American Academy of Arts and Letters for the best work of fiction published during the previous five years. (In accepting, Cheever wondered with characteristic acuity about the wisdom of dividing American fiction into half-decade periods.) All along he has been a writer's writer, admired by such fellow craftsmen as John Gardner, John Hersey, Joan Didion, George Garrett, and Joseph Heller. Someone once referred to John Updike as his disciple, a classification that ignores both the independent achievements of each man and the real friendship between them.

Cheever's work refuses to fit comfortably into any critical pigeonhole, a fact that is demonstrated by the variety of writers to whom he has been compared. He has reminded some, for example, of such social observers as Marquand and O'Hara, a categorization he repudiates: "The fact that I can count the olives in a dish just as quick as John O'Hara doesn't mean that I am O'Hara." He has been likened to Nabokov for their mutual capacity to turn the cultural artifacts of contemporary life to artistic purposes. He resembles Fitzgerald, it has been asserted, for the luminosity of his prose and for that "extraordinary gift for hope," that "romantic readiness" that he shares with Jay Gatsby. In the best work of both writers, one always knows "what time it is, precisely where you are, the kind of country." "If he has a master," Elizabeth Hardwick observed, "it is probably F. Scott Fitzgerald."

John Cheever

Cheever has been called the "Chekhov of the suburbs," and is most like the Russian master, perhaps, in his knack for making patently ridiculous characters seem somehow winning. He has been compared to Hawthorne for possessing a sense of history—an awareness not merely of the pastness of the past, but of the pastness in the present. He is like Faulkner, it has been observed, in bringing to life a particular plot of American ground—the New York suburb, rather than the Mississippi county. And he seems like Kafka to yet another reader, for in their fiction the shadow of the sinister can fall across the outwardly commonplace landscape in the blink of an eye. Indeed, the multiplicity of such comparisons suggests that Cheever is right in denying that he belongs to any particular American literary tradition, other than the abiding one of individuality.

There is general agreement about Cheever's shortcomings. He is better at the particular scene than at stringing scenes together. His tightly wrought short stories are generally superior to the novels, which tend toward the episodic in their looseness of structure; and perhaps because of Yankee reticence, he has not always plumbed the depths of his characters. He inveighs against contemporary ills—the standardization of culture, the decline in sexual mores that tends to confuse love with lust, the obliteration of nature by the engines of technology—but blurs his outrage with blue-sky endings.

Cheever's merits far outweigh such shortcomings, however. He has achieved an "amazing precision of style and language," and is capable of lyrical moments reminiscent, once again, of Fitzgerald. He possesses "a remarkably acute nose" for the fascinating situation, "a remarkably acute ear" for the thing said in context. Memory and imagination are blended into a remarkable comic inventiveness. His genius is the "genius of place." His greatest gift is "for entering the minds of men and women at crucial moments." No other writer "tells us so much"—this from Didion—"about the way we live now." Furthermore, he is not for nothing a descendant of the Puritans, and his writing is invariably grounded on firm moral bedrock.

Cheever knows that fiction is not meant to provide lessons, but "to illuminate, to explode, to refresh." Still, the journeys his characters undertake are fraught with moral perils, and he judges those who fall by the wayside according to conventional and traditional standards. Those led astray are inflexibly punished, banished from enjoyment of the natural world that lies around them. But he is an "enlightened

Puritan" of the twentieth century; and for him the greatest, most saving virtues are those he wishes for in himself and his children: love and usefulness.

Cheever finds solace in his work; and his greatest pleasure comes in shutting himself off in a room to get a story down on paper. At such moments he feels he is practicing his rightful calling. For when writing, he is invested by a ". . . sense of total usefulness. We all have a power of control, it's part of our lives; we have it in love, in work that we love doing. It's a sense of ecstasy, as simple as that. The sense is that 'this is my usefulness, and I can do it all the way through.'"

Beyond the Cheeveresque: A Style Both Lyrical and Idiosyncratic

*George Hunt**

John Cheever has won many awards for his fiction, but the praise and prizes have been reserved for his four excellent novels, *The Wapshot Chronicle, The Wapshot Scandal, Bullet Park*, and *Falconer*. Short stories, by contrast, rarely win important prizes, and collections of stories do not sell well. Cheever persists nonetheless in this neglected *genre*, which he terms "the literature of the nomad." *The Stories of John Cheever*, a handsomely designed and printed edition of 61 stories, represents his greatest achievement.

For too long critics have been idly content with the clichés "Cheever country" and "Cheeveresque," a reviewer's shorthand betraying a sensibility less wide and deep than the author's own. Cheever country has become synonymous with the suburbs that abut Route 95 from New York to Boston, a homogenized landscape of semi-elegant cook-outs, drained pools in the winter, parties that begin "Oh, *do* come" and end with forlorn or frantic goodbyes, a place peopled by an upper crust, now moldly or pulpy with desperation, fits of sexual tension, or mere silliness. The implication is that Cheever is something of a sociologist in disguise, a wry and macabre David Riesman who delights in count-

*From *Commonweal* 106 (19 January 1979), 20–22. Reprinted with permission of the Commonweal Foundation.

ing the olives in drained martini glasses or the soggy shards of charcoal at aborted cook-outs.

But Cheever is not a sociologist; he is an artist. A social scientist's concern is to so concentrate on particular instances that, accumulatively, a general pattern for understanding the behavior of some segment of society might emerge. The artist, too, begins with the concrete particular, but he *enters* it; a particular experience is thus transformed by his imaginative and compassionate feeling in order that the humanly universal, not the statistically general, might emerge and engage our feeling and imaginative response. The findings of the social sciences are, almost by definition, statable. The results of art elude such definition since the art of fiction, at its best, engages mystery, the mystery of the human and its corollary, the mystery of language.

These twin mysteries are the key to the magic of John Cheever. As this collection demonstrates, the thematic *what* of his fiction is far broader than that of the vicissitudes of megapolis's upper middle class. His central characters range from elevator man to well-digger; the locales include Italy and Russia; and the emotions are rhapsodic and celebratory as often as sad. The recurring place-names like St. Botolphs, Shady Hill, Bullet Park are imaginative constructs not social symbols; they are more and less than places on a map. They are, as Cheever has said, "metaphors for human confinement," whether the confinement be that of nostalgia or tradition, or erotic entanglements or of our universal perception of being both travelers and pilgrims and "stuck" somehow, trapped by conflicting aspirations above and below.

That thematic *what*, of course, Cheever shares with many contemporary writers; his distinction lies in the artistic *how*, in his remarkably graceful and lucid prose. We respond to the verbal rhythms of our other two most elegant and versatile stylists, John Updike and Saul Bellow, *inside* our heads. Both Updike and Bellow, though, are difficult to read aloud for a sustained period; Cheever's prose almost demands that it be read aloud. It comes as no surprise, then, to learn in his charming preface to this collection that a good deal of these stories were composed that way and tested with his family as critical audience. Cheever's prose edges closer to the cadences of modern poetry than that of any of his contemporaries.

Cheever's style is both lyrical and idiosyncratic. When lyrical, it is reminiscent of the later poetry of W. B. Yeats and, when idiosyncratic, of the later W. H. Auden. Cheever's stories, in fact, engage many Yeatsian themes: the passion for decorum and ceremonies of innocence

133

in the face of the drowning of decay and disruption; the contrast of man's urge for the "higher" beauties of the artistic and natural order with his lower impulses like the sexually chaotic and the murderous; those emotions of manic desperation that accompany one's realization of aging and its consequence, death. Stylistically, Cheever continually uses the later Yeats technique of direct address to the reader. This technique brings to a story a unique dramatic force; the voice is unabashedly personal and we as readers are encountered, willynilly, by someone grabbing us by the lapels. A good number of his stories begin this way: the voice announces that he is a writer and the variations in his tone of voice prepare us (or so we think) for what will follow—but we had better listen or else. The range possible with this technique is remarkable and Cheever exploits it at the beginning of the following stories:

"The Ocean"—a conspiratorial voice: "I am keeping this journal because I believe myself to be in some danger and because I have no other way of recording my fears."

"The Death of Justina"—a complaint: "So help me God it gets more and more preposterous, it corresponds less and less to what I remember and what I expect. . . ."

"Percy"—quaintly philosophical: "Reminiscence, along with the cheeseboards and ugly pottery sometimes given to brides, seems to have a manifest destiny with the sea."

"The Brigadier and the Golf Widow"—apologetic and inquisitive: "I would not want to be one of those writers who begin each morning by exclaiming, 'O Gogol, O Checkhov, O Thackeray and Dickens, what would you have made of a bomb shelter ornamented with four plaster-of-Paris ducks, a birdbath, and three composition gnomes with long beards and red mobcaps?'"

In addition, there are throughout these stories the Yeatsian long lyric line, iambic in rhythm, merging the abstract impulse with the concrete detail. This is Francis Weed's vision in Cheever's masterpiece, "The Country Husband." "Up through the dimness of his mind rose the image of the mountain deep in snow. It was late in the day. Wherever his eyes looked, he saw broad and heartening things. Over his shoulder, there was a snow-filled valley, rising into wooded hills where the trees dimmed the whiteness like a sparse coat of hair."

But Yeats was never funny, at least deliberately, and it is here that Cheever parts from Yeats and joins Auden. Like Auden, Cheever is not a satirist, though it might seem so. Instead, he is what Kierkegaard called a "humorist," one whose compassionate understanding of the human comedy with its absurd enthusiasms and low-life urgencies forestalls in his heart the easy, mocking perspective of facile satire. Neither Cheever nor Auden expect or desire a radical change in the human condition, they are content to embrace it, whole and not piecemeal, despite a knowing eye. Is not this Audenesque and Cheeveresque? "We admire decency and we despise death, but even the mountains seem to shift in the space of a night and perhaps the exhibitionist at the corner of Chestnut and Elm streets is more significant than the lovely woman with a bar of sunlight in her hair, putting a fresh piece of cuttlebone in the nightingale's cage."

Like Auden, Cheever's comic technique will entail: a continual and abrupt shifting of stylistic gears from fantasy to realism, a seeming solemnity of tone that suddenly issues in the mock-heroic catching us unawares, the old juxtaposition of different items in a list, with the last detail a comic climax, a blurring switch from the banal to the shocking and a return to the banal. Throughout, as in Auden, the narrator's voice is ever decorous, detached, urbane; but its tone is never "tsk-tsk," rather it is "well, what do *we* know" and "wait, there's even more to tell."

Fortunately, in Cheever there is always more to tell, and the fertility of his imagination is extraordinary. One critic has described Cheever's style with disfavor as "episodic notation" in that his narratives move swiftly and almost in linear fashion from one glimpse, one incident, one snippet of conversation to another. What is sacrificed here in terms of organic fictional unity—always the stuffy critic's touchstone when he has little else to say—is redeemed by exceptional inventiveness, flexibility and versatility. This apparently loose structure gives his stories the qualities of a yarn and, *sans* dialect and sentimentality, places him firmly in the American tradition of Mark Twain, Ring Lardner and Damon Runyon. Furthermore, a Cheever dialogue is unique in that, while it remains true to our realistic ear, it is always heightened beyond realism to a peculiar brand of poetic speech—and it is this that sets him apart from the genial accuracy of a John O'Hara or Philip Roth.

Finally, the acid test of the comic: Cheever is consistently hilarious. Alone with Peter De Vries's best efforts, Cheever's fiction is not meant to be read among strangers, on planes or trains where suddenly laughing out loud might be thought unseemly or worse. Here, for example, is one narrator's summary account of his eccentric Aunt Percy's marriage: "Percy and Abbott Tracy met in some such place, and she fell in love. He had already begun a formidable and clinical sexual career, and seemed unacquainted in any way with sentiment, although I recall that he liked to watch children saying their prayers. Percy listened for his footsteps, she languished in his absence, his cigar cough sounded to her like music, and she filled a portfolio with pencil sketches of his face, his eyes, his hands, and, after their marriage, the rest of him. . . ."

Just as Cheever is not a strict satirist he is not a moralist either. And yet, his work, as his last novel *Falconer* made evident, is deeply Christian in sensibility. Few of his stories, apart from cleverly inserted Biblical allusions, are obviously religious in design. But Cheever's sympathy with his characters' fallen state together with their vague yearnings for personal rebirth, for a virtuous life possibly untrammeled by life's more sordid confusions, betray his sincere Episcopal beliefs. Every artist's endeavor demands an implicit faith-commitment to a world he hopes will reward it, but Cheever has been more religiously specific. He has said in an interview, "The religious experience is very much my concern, as it seems to me it is the legitimate concern of any adult who has experienced love. . . . The whiteness of light. In the church, you know, that always represents the Holy Spirit. It seems to me that man's inclination toward light, toward brightness, is very nearly botanical—and I mean spiritual light. One not only needs it, one struggles for it. It seems to be that one's total experience is the drive toward light."

Unfortunately, despite that inviting light, we are *here* and not there; yet, Cheever, like all great artists consciously committed to religious faith or otherwise, begins here. No other short story in my memory captures better what theologians have called the mystery of Original Sin than his excellent "Seaside Houses." In the story, the narrator, a gentle and reasonable man, has rented a summer cottage for his family. Gradually, he realizes that the Greenwoods who had rented the cottage the previous summer have left ominous moral baggage behind. The narrator discovers a boy's scrawl, "My father is a rat," hidden on a corner baseboard; caches of empty whiskey bottles are found; obscene gossip is later heard about the Greenwoods; soon the narrator begins to dream dreams that he realizes are Mr. Greenwood's dreams. Suddenly, Mr. Greenwood's presence begins to infect him, destroying his relationship with his wife and family. Greenwood has become his counterpart, he divorces, and the story ends with this reflection of his in another seaside house with another wife: "The shore is curved, and I can see the lights of other haunted cottages where people are building up an accrual of happiness or misery that will be left for the August tenants or the people who come next year. Are we truly this close to one another? Must we impose our burdens on strangers? And is our sense of the universality of suffering so inescapable?"

Perhaps those last lines sound faintly cosmic or even pompous, but it is a generous risk that Cheever takes. The other risk is the risk to be hilarious, a risk that the truly pompous regard as lightweight. Like life itself, humor has no weight, only intensity. No one without a sense of humor can deeply enjoy any other of the myriad of human sensations; sadly, for those without, humor and its acolytes offer not mystery but endless mystification. But humor, certainly as often as tragedy, shocks us into truth. Cheever does this again and again; as he has said, "We can cherish nothing less than our random understanding of death and the earth-shaking love that draws us to one another."

From Parallels to Paradise: The Lyrical Structure of Cheever's Fiction

*Robert Morace**

The first point to be made concerning the structure of Cheever's stories is that while most of them are not as improvisational and devoid of plot as Cheever would like us to believe, neither is linear development of primary importance. This is evident even in Cheever's first published story, "Expelled" (1930), where the nonlinear structure has sometimes been misread as a sign of literary apprenticeship rather than understood as characteristic of Cheever's approach, both early and late, to the writing of fiction. The story's five sections—untitled introduction, "The Colonel," "Margaret Courtright," "Laura Driscoll," and "Five Months Later"—are not discrete sketches that never quite come together in the form of a single harmonious short story; rather, they constitute the planes and angular perceptions of an art that is, for all its comforting realism, very nearly cubist in effect. Many of Cheever's

*Excerpted from an article (same title) to be published in the Winter 1989 issue of *Twentieth Century Literature*. By permission of William McBrien, editor.

later stories, in particular the ones most often anthologized as short story classics, do proceed in linear fashion, but the progress through time and the more or less straightforward plot of these stories is deceptive. "The Enormous Radio" (1947), "Torch Song" (1947), "O Youth and Beauty" (1953), and "The Swimmer" (1964), for example, are written in a prose equivalent of the device used in many folk ballads, incremental repetition. Essentially, Cheever plays the same scene or situation over and over with slight but cumulatively significant changes, gradually transforming the real into the fantastic, time into dream. This is obvious enough in the case of a story such as "The Swimmer," in which the parallelism is so insistent, the story's structure (and pace) very clearly following the order (and speed) of Neddy Merrill's pool-to-pool odyssey. In most of Cheever's stories and in all of his novels the parallelism is less insistent and, therefore, less obvious, though no less integral to the individual work's effectiveness and to Cheever's art—Moses' encounters with his boss, his doctor, and his mayor in "The Death of Justina" (1960), for example. It is not plot that makes these stories so effective but the author's skillful, perhaps even intuitive use of parallel elements.

What Roman Jakobson has said of the structure of poetry applies equally well to the structure of Cheever's stories and novels: "In poetry similarity [metaphor] is imposed on contiguity [metonymic plot], and hence equivalence is promoted to the constitutive device of the sequence." It is precisely in those works in which the metaphoric parallelism is muted and therefore not self-consciously placed before the reader that Cheever's poetic technique has most often been misunderstood and judged as evidence of structural weakness, an aberration from the sequential plot that is the Aristotelian soul of conventional fiction. The Gertrude Flannery scene in "The Country Husband," for example, like the Gertrude Lockhart passage in *The Wapshot Scandal*, is not, as Lynne Waldeland has charged, disproportionate and without any thematic purpose; rather, little Gertrude's situation as stray parallels the protagonist's, Francis's, situation as "weed" in his suburban Garden of Eden. Similarly, the John Barth–like authorial intrusion near the end of "Boy in Rome" is entirely appropriate to Cheever's purpose in that both the homesick boy in Rome and the author-narrator in Ossining are exiles yearning for that elusive America of the soul where they hope to find relief from their "incurable loneliness." Each voice— the author's and the boy-narrator's—echoes and deepens the other, transforming the individual plaint into a song of universal longing. This striving for the universal is by no means peculiar to Cheever's work; rather, it is, as the humanists like to say, the aim of all art. Nonetheless, it does point to a certain expansiveness that does distinguish Cheever's stories insofar as it is very much at odds with the compression of incident and tight narrative focus that are the hallmarks of the conventional short story. An assiduous observer of the unities Cheever is not, for in the space of just ten or fifteen pages, he will make use of a variety of geographical settings, an unusually large cast of characters, and/or a surprisingly lengthy period of time (weeks, months, even years, as in "Torch Song" and "The Children").

A relatively early work, "The Common Day" (1947), illustrates very well one phase of Cheever's expansive approach to fiction-writing. The story's spatial and temporal settings are quite specific: the New Hampshire countryside, a summer's day. The focus on character is much less precise. Although there is a central figure, Jim Brown, the story cannot be said to be about him in the same way "The Swimmer," for example, is about Neddy Merrill or Hawthorne's "Young Goodman Brown" is about its protagonist. In fact, Cheever's Brown is not a protagonist in any usual sense because the focus of this story is not on any one character but, instead, on what all ten characters have in "common," their sense of geographical and psychological dislocation. A city dweller and the head of his own family, Jim feels uncomfortable and out of place while on a visit to the country estate of his mother-in-law, Mrs. Garrison, "the rightful owner of all he could see" (*SJC*, 22). So do the hired help—all of them foreign-born—whom Mrs. Garrison appears to tyrannize. Jim's son, Timmy, finds himself neglected by the Irish nurse, Agnes Shay, who lavishes all her attention on four-year-old Carlotta, "her only link with the morning, with the sun, with everything beautiful and exciting" (25). This is not a story about the successful forging of "links," however, or about the ties that bind. Agnes is rebuffed by Carlotta who, seeking admission to the adult world of her grandmother, is in turn rebuffed by Mrs. Garrison, who for all her wealth and power feels no more at ease or at home than her granddaughter, her son-in-law, or her servants. These characters share the same physical space, the same common day, and the same sense of estrangement, yet what the reader feels most acutely is the vast emotional distance that separates each from the others. Jim longs to return to the safety of his home in the city; his wife, Ellen, on the other hand, yearns for a country place of her own, for only there, she believes, will she ever feel secure. In their case, the emotional distance appears ready to widen until it is as great as the gulf which separates the servants from their European homelands, Mrs. Garrison from her youth and from her dead husband, and Carlotta from the mother who, we are told, "had gone West to get a divorce that summer" (24). The sense of separation and dislocation that plays an important thematic role in "The Common Day" and other Cheever fictions has an equally important bearing on the structural unity of these works, as will soon be made clear. Suffice it to say at this point that this unity depends considerably less on linear plot, narrative focus, and character development than it does on various forms of narrative parallelism: echoing, juxtaposition, counterpoint, incremental repetition, thematic variations, and the coming together of disparate characters, situations, and narrative lines.

Significantly, during the time Cheever was writing the novels his reviewers and critics have faulted for being too much like Cheever's stories, he was writing a collection of stories very nearly novelistic in effect (*The Housebreaker of Shady Hill*, 1958) and composing short fictions that were becoming more and more discontinuous: the comic-opera narration of "The Day the Pig Fell in the Well" (1954); the multiple narratives of "The Trouble with Marcie Flint" (1957); the four parallel stories in "The Bella Lingua" (1958); the decidedly and ironically linear plot of "Montraldo" (1964), in which the order of events fails to yield any meaning other than the rule of chance in a discontinuous world; the free association technique of "The Jewels of the Cabots" (1972); and finally the rambling, indeed literally peripatetic, narrative of Cheever's most chaotic and perhaps most autobiographical story, "The President of the Argentine" (1976). "The Day the Pig Fell in the Well" is especially noteworthy in that, appearing just three years before the publication of *The Wapshot Chronicle* in 1957, it is a literary hybrid, a short story which is, in fact, a compressed novel. Far more than "The Common Day," it dramatically evidences that fondness for "incidental narrative" and "stretching of the conventional rules," which have become two of Cheever's trademarks.

In the summer, when the Nudd family gathered at Whitebeach Camp in the Adirondacks, there was always a night when one of them would ask, "Remember the day the pig fell in the well?" Then, as if the opening note of a sextet had been sounded, the others would all rush in to take their familiar parts, like those families who sing Gilbert and Sullivan, and the recital would go on for an hour or more. The perfect days—and there had been hundreds of them—seemed to have passed into their consciousness without a memory, and they returned to this chronicle of small disasters as if it were the genesis of summer. (*SJC*, 219)

This opening paragraph is, like Cheever's title, a bit misleading, for the story told *by* the Nudds constitutes only a part of Cheever's story *of* the Nudds. Read in one way, the narrative of the day the pig fell in the well is nothing more than a plot contrivance, an excuse for telling a number of loosely connected anecdotes: "The summer the pig fell in the well was also Esther's tennis summer and the summer that she became so thin" (220). Read another way, it serves as the central point from which the various "incidental," or parallel, narratives abruptly radiate and to which they eventually return, just as the Nudds return each summer to their "seasonal paradise" in the Adirondacks. Insofar as Cheever's story repeatedly folds back upon itself in the process of its telling, telescoping thirty or so summers into a vaguely defined past, "The Day the Pig Fell in the Well" cannot be said to develop along conventional lines, from conflict through climax to resolution. Instead of developing plot and character, Cheever deepens the mood and increases the emotional intensity, and herein lies the remarkable effectiveness not only of this particular story but of his fiction in general.

The story begins as comedy; there are slapstick accidents, absurdly funny misunderstandings, and a plot so wayward that even death—the pig's—evokes laughter. Then, almost imperceptibly, the mood begins to darken. A father's problems with his business partners, a daughter's divorce, a son's death—mere footnotes at first—gradually grow in importance until they nearly overwhelm the Nudds, whose cartoonish names suddenly seem so inappropriate to their roles in the domestic tragedy that Cheever's story has become. Against the economic and political vicissitudes of their world, Cheever posits the permanence of their "seasonal paradise": "There had been the boom, the crash, the depression, the recession, the malaise of imminent war, the war itself, the boom, the inflation, the recession, the slump, and now there was the malaise again, but none of this had changed a stone or a leaf in the view she [Mrs. Nudd] saw from her porch" (234). Similarly, against the tragic discontinuity of their lives, Cheever posits the comic discontinuity of the story of the day the pig fell in the well. More than a plot contrivance, a thin narrative thread, their "chronicle of small disasters" serves both as an alternative to the personal tragedies they have had to endure and as a substitute for a religious faith they no longer possess.

Appropriately, it is Mrs. Nudd, who, as Cheever carefully points out, "had no more faith in the power of God than she had in the magic of the evening star" (231), who invokes the power of fiction to dispel the tragic gloom that has settled over Whitebeach, speaking near the end of Cheever's story the same ritualistic invocation which had been heard at its beginning: "Remember the day the pig fell in the well?" (219, 235). Bereft of their place in the world of wars and depressions (both economic and psychological), "they all waited graciously for their turn" (235), taking refuge and comfort in the communal telling of their tale: "The story restored Mrs. Nudd and made her feel that all was well. It had exhilarated the rest, and, talking loudly and laughing, they went into the house. Mr. Nudd lighted a fire and sat down to play checkers with Joan. Mrs. Nudd passed a box of stale candy. It had begun to blow outside, and the house creaked gently, like a hull when the wind takes up the sail" (235). It is not only the Nudds whom the story restores and exhilarates, but the reader, too, who has perhaps been lulled into forgetting that Cheever's story is not single but double. So is Cheever's ending. In a final sentence, Cheever takes back all that the preceding few paragraphs have restored. "The room with the people in it looked enduring and secure, although in the morning they would all be gone." The result is akin to what the poststructuralists like to call a self-cancelling or self-deconstructing text, which frustrates the reader-critic's efforts to extract any univocal meaning. As in so many of Cheever's works, the "meaning" of "The Day the Pig Fell in the Well" does not derive from the author's resolution of the dramatic conflict he has set in motion; it derives instead from the tension Cheever creates by pitting various parallel elements, including characters, scenes, and moods, against each other. "That late in the season, the light went quickly. It was sunny one minute and dark the next" (234).

The characters in this and other Cheever fictions all face the same problem: how to live in a world that, in spite of all its middle-class comforts and assurances, suddenly appears inhospitable, even dangerous, a world that appears to be growing more and more incoherent and "preposterous" every day, one in which the "moral chain of being" has become a mere "thread" and where—as the audience for contemporary art, music, and fiction knows all too well—it is becoming increasingly difficult "to distinguish persiflage from profundity." Cheever the author faces a similar problem: how to write about such a world in a way that will take account of the incoherence without succumbing to it.

Cheever addresses the problem directly in the prologue to "The Death of Justina": "Fiction is art and art is the triumph over chaos (no less) and we can accomplish this only by the most vigilant exercise of choice, but in a world that changes more swiftly than we can perceive there is always the danger that our powers of selection will be mistaken and that the vision we serve will come to nothing" (429). The discontinuities of stories such as "The Death of Justina," "The Day the Pig Fell in the Well," and "The President of the Argentine" can, however, be traced to a more personal cause than that vague standby, the chaos of the modern era. When asked in an interview with John Hersey to explain if he could the "blurted quality" of his writings, Cheever attributed it to "some ungainliness in my spiritual person that I cannot master." If *Falconer* and *Oh What A Paradise It Seems* come closer to satisfying the demands of his more traditional reviewers and critics, it is not because they are structured any differently than the stories, the Wapshot books, and *Bullet Park* (they are not), but because in them Cheever comes closer to mastering his sense of spiritual ungainliness. And the most palpable evidence of this mastery is to be found in the triumph of Cheever's narrative voice.

Cheever's distinctive narrative voice has already received considerable attention and has in fact been identified by a number of reviewers and critics as *the* unifying element in the fiction. We can, however, go further, for this voice which seems to balance so effortlessly and yet precariously between the earthly and spiritual realms, between satire and celebration, detachment and compassion, irony and lyricism (its most salient feature) appears to have come into existence only as Cheever began to write *The Wapshot Chronicle*. (As late as 1953, reviewers of *The Enormous Radio and Other Stories* were still commenting on Cheever's "deliberately flat, controlled style.") A careful reading of this novel suggests that he may have discovered his distinctive voice—and the need for it—in order to offset those images of quagmire, torn sky, and the American inferno that dominated his thinking in the 1950s and that continued to trouble him at least until the writing of *Falconer* in 1975. As Cheever confided in his journal as late as 1974, "That bridge of language, metaphor, anecdote and imagination that I build each morning to cross the incongruities in my life seems very frail indeed." Even before he perfected his distinctive lyrical style as a frail bridge between discontinuous fact and harmonious vision, Cheever had often appended self-consciously lyrical passages to a number of his stories, including "The Country Husband": "Then it is dark; it is a night where kings in golden suits ride elephants over the mountains" (*SJC*, 346).

Such passages attach themselves to Cheever's stories ambiguously, reflecting the author's own ambivalence concerning the validity of the transcendent vision that his lyricism implies. The lyrical endings soar above the confinements and frustrations of the protagonists' lives, yet the loftiness of the language and the seeming inappropriateness of the vision to the rest of the story make the lyricism suspect. Cheever seems both to affirm the vision and to mock it, as well as the author-character who would conjure it out of nothing but his own desire and imagination. This same ambivalence characterized Cheever the man—"Life for my father," Susan Cheever has noted, "was either unbearable or transcendent"—and Cheever the author—"In the later fiction," R. G. Collins has cogently argued, "Cheever seems to be suspended between a tragic pessimism and a raptured expectancy; he writes as an impaled victim believing that, somewhere near, there sounds unearthly salvation; he seems to be listening for the angels, as the earth smoulders beneath him." Cheever did not wait for the angelic choir to begin its song; he chose instead to sing it himself, doing for his readers and himself what the girl does for the narrator in "The Angel of the Bridge": to sing them over the incongruities of their world and over the abyss of spiritual ungainliness and unfulfilled longing. I use the word "song" here in a literal as well as figurative sense, for the development of Cheever's lyrical style and his less guarded acceptance of the transcendent vision it implies necessitated the development of a less factually realistic and more nearly musical prose.

When, in the 1947 story "The Enormous Radio," Cheever referred to the machine's "mistaken sensitivity to discord" (*SJC*, 34), he was being doubly ironic. The radio's "sensitivity to discord" is mistaken from the point of view of the apartment dwellers who would prefer to hide their bickerings, anxieties, and abortions behind the facade of middle-class respectability. It is also mistaken from the point of view of Cheever's lyricism, the goal of which is not discord but concord and a special kind of "decorum." As Cheever learned from his *New Yorker* editor, Harold Ross, "Decorum is a mode of speech, as profound and connotative as any other, differing not in content but in syntax and imagery" (*SJC*, viii). I have already noted that the structure of Cheever's fictions is based on the use of parallel elements metaphorically juxtaposed on the basis of similarity rather than either causality or spatiotemporal contiguity. Cheever's sentences are similarly constructed and combined—for example, "There were no preliminaries this time. The seizure came with a rush. The strength went out of my legs, I gasped for breath, and felt the terrifying loss of sight" (*SJC*, 495–96), where the structure is decidedly paratactic, and "How can a people who do not mean to understand death hope to understand life and who will sound the alarm" (*SJC*, 437), which may look like prose but which sounds like poetry:

> How can a people
> > who do not mean to understand death
> > > hope to understand life
> > and who will sound the alarm?

Partly elegaic, partly humorous, but always decorously balanced, the lyrical style enables Cheever to satirize his characters and at the same time to rise above the satire in order to read the often trivial signs of the times in terms of what they connote figuratively and spiritually rather than what they denote literally and socioeconomically.

Such a style is transitional in a double sense. It serves as the vital and necessary link between the seemingly separate yet interpenetrating realms of the literal/prosaic and the visionary/poetic, and it is a style that is itself in transition. Over the course of his career and especially during the period that his fiction became increasingly discontinuous, Cheever became less concerned with providing factual information about the "practical world" (*SJC*, 337) and more concerned with evoking a lyrical mood.

Chronology

1912   John Cheever born 27 May to Frederick and Mary Cheever in Quincy, Massachusetts.

1926–1929   Attends Quincy High School and Thayer Academy, South Braintree, Mass.

1929   Expelled from Thayer.

1930   "Expelled," a fictional account of his experience at Thayer, appears in 1 October *New Republic.*

1930–1934   Continues to write; leaves home to live with brother Fred in Boston.

1931   Travels through Europe with Fred.

1934   Moves to New York. Visits Yaddo, artists' retreat in Saratoga, New York. Works at various jobs to support himself.

1935   Publishes his first *New Yorker* story, "Brooklyn Rooming House," 25 May.

1939   Meets Mary Winternitz.

1941   Marries Mary Winternitz, 22 March.

1942   Inducted into U.S. Army in May; trains as an infantryman in South Carolina and Georgia. Starts a series of "army life" stories.

1943   *The Way Some People Live,* first short story collection, published in March. Daughter Susan born 31 July. Cheever transferred to Signal Corps and becomes military film script writer.

1945   Sent to the Philippines on assignment in the spring. Honorably discharged in November.

1946–1950   Lives in New York; experiments with humor and fantasy in several stories, including "The Enormous Radio"; tries and fails to write a novel.

1947   "The Enormous Radio" and other innovative stories published by the *New Yorker.*

1948   Son Benjamin born 4 May.

1951   Moves from New York City to Scarborough, New York. Awarded Guggenheim grant.

1953   *The Enormous Radio and Other Stories* published in February.

1954–1956   Teaches writing at Barnard College; works on *The Wapshot Chronicle*.

1955   "The Five-Forty-Eight" receives Benjamin Franklin Award.

1956   Receives O. Henry Award for "The Country Husband." Travels to Italy for year-long stay with Mary and the children.

1957   In Italy. Son Federico born 9 March. *The Wapshot Chronicle* published in March; elected to the National Institute of Arts and Letters.

1958   *The Wapshot Chronicle* wins National Book Award. Third major story collection, *The Housebreaker of Shady Hill*, published in September.

1960   Receives second Guggenheim grant, to work on another novel.

1961   Moves to Ossining, New York. *Some People, Places and Things That Will Not Appear in My Next Novel* appears in April.

1964   Second novel, *The Wapshot Scandal*, published in January. *The Brigadier and the Golf Widow* (short stories) published in October. Travels to Russia as part of a cultural exchange; forms lasting friendship there with John Updike.

1965   *The Wapshot Scandal* wins Howells Medal of the American Academy of Arts and Letters.

1968   "The Swimmer" appears as a Frank and Eleanor Perry film.

1969   *Bullet Park* published in April, to mixed reviews.

1971–1972   Teaches writing to Sing Sing prison inmates.

1973   *The World of Apples* published in May. Teaches at University of Iowa Writers Workshop. Elected to the American Academy of Arts and Letters.

1974   Hired to teach at Boston University; becomes seriously alcoholic and depressed.

1975   Treated in Boston and (successfully) in New York for alcoholism. Works strenuously on novel about prison life.

1977   *Falconer* published to generally favorable reviews; Cheever's life and work featured in *Newsweek* magazine, 14 March.

1978   Given honorary doctorate from Harvard. *The Stories of John Cheever* published in November.

1979   Receives Pulitzer Prize and National Book Critics Circle award for *The Stories of John Cheever.*

1980   Suffers grand mal seizure while at Yaddo.

1981   *The Stories of John Cheever* given American Book Award. In July, cancer discovered during kidney surgery.

1982   Novella *Oh What a Paradise It Seems* published in March. Receives National Medal for Literature in April. Dies in Ossining, 18 June; buried in Norwell, Massachusetts.

Selected Bibliography

Primary Works

Collections of Short Fiction

The Brigadier and the Golf Widow. New York: Harper & Row, 1964; reprint, New York: Bantam, 1965. "The Brigadier and the Golf Widow," "The Angel of the Bridge," "An Educated American Woman," "The Swimmer," "Metamorphoses," "The Bella Lingua," "Clementina," "A Woman without a Country," "Reunion," "The Chaste Clarissa," "The Music Teacher," "The Seaside Houses," "Just One More Time," "Marito in Città," "A Vision of the World," "The Ocean."

The Enormous Radio and Other Stories. New York: Funk & Wagnalls, 1953; reprint, New York, Harper & Row, Colophon, 1965. "Goodbye, My Brother," "The Pot of Gold," "O City of Broken Dreams," "The Children," "Torch Song," "The Cure," "The Hartleys," "The Summer Farmer," "The Superintendent," "The Enormous Radio," "The Season of Divorce," "Christmas Is a Sad Season for the Poor," "The Sutton Place Story," "Clancy in the Tower of Babel."

Homage to Shakespeare. Limited hardcover reprint of story. Stevenson, Conn.: Country Squire Books, 1968.

The Housebreaker of Shady Hill and Other Stories. New York: Harper & Brothers, 1958; reprint, New York: Macfadden Books, 1961. "The Housebreaker of Shady Hill," "O Youth and Beauty!," "The Country Husband," "The Sorrows of Gin," "The Worm in the Apple," "The Five-Forty-Eight," "Just Tell Me Who It Was," "The Trouble of Marcie Flint."

Some People, Places, and Things That Will Not Appear in My Next Novel. New York: Harper & Brothers, 1961; reprint, New York: Bantam, 1963. "The Death of Justina," "Brimmer," "The Lowboy," "The Duchess," "The Scarlet Moving Van," "The Golden Age," "The Wrysons," "Boy in Rome," "A Miscellany of Characters That Will Not Appear."

The Stories of John Cheever. New York: Alfred A. Knopf, 1978; reprint, New York: Ballantine Books, 1980. A retrospective collection containing the stories listed for earlier anthologies except *The Way Some People Live*, with "The Common Day," "The Day the Pig Fell into the Well," "The Bus to St. James's," and "Another Story" added.

The Uncollected Stories of John Cheever, 1930–1981. Chicago: Academy Chicago, (expected) 1989. "Expelled," "Fall River," "Late Gathering," "Bock

Beer and Bermuda Onions," "Brooklyn Rooming House," "Buffalo,"
"The Autobiography of a Drummer," "In Passing," "Bayonne," "Play a
March," "The Princess," "A Picture for the Home," "Behold a Cloud in
the West," "Homage to Shakespeare," "The Teaser," "In the Begin-
ning," "His Young Wife," "Frère Jacques," "Saratoga," "Treat," "The
Happiest Days," "It's Hot in Egypt," "The Man She Loved," "I'm
Going to Asia," "A Present for Louisa," "A Bird in the Hand," "From
This Day Forward," "The Pursuit of Happiness," "A Place of Great His-
torical Interest," "Family Dinner," "Sergeant Limeburner," "They Shall
Inherit the Earth," "A Tale of Old Pennsylvania," "The Invisible Ship,"
"My Friends and Neighbors All, Farewell," "Dear Lord, We Thank
Thee for Thy Bounty," "Somebody Has to Die," "A Walk in the Park,"
"The Single Purpose of Leon Burrows," "The Mouth of the Turtle,"
"Town House," "Manila," "Town House II," "A Trip to the Moon,"
"Town House III," "Town House IV," "Town House V," "Town House
VI," "Love in the Islands," "The Beautiful Mountains," "Roseheath,"
"The Opportunity," "Keep the Ball Rolling," "The Temptations of
Emma Boynton," "Vega," "The Reasonable Music," "The People You
Meet," "The National Pastime," "The True Confessions of Henry Pell,"
"The Journal of a Writer with a Hole in One Sock," "How Dr. Wareham
Kept His Servants," "Paola," "The Events of That Easter," "The Habit,"
"President of the Argentine," "The Night Mummy Got the Wrong Mink
Coat," "The Island." (Exact contents to be determined.)

The Way Some People Live. New York: Random House, 1943. "Summer The-
atre," "Forever Hold Your Peace," "In the Eyes of God," "The Pleasures
of Solitude," "Cat," "Summer Remembered," "Of Love: A Testimony,"
"The Edge of the World," "Hello, Dear," "Happy Birthday, Enid,"
"Run, Sheep, Run," "The Law of the Jungle," "North of Portland,"
"Washington Boarding House," "Riding Stable," "Survivor," "Tomorrow
Is a Beautiful Day," "There They Go," "The Shape of a Night," "The
Brothers," "Publick House," "When Grandmother Goes," "A Border In-
cident," "The New World," "These Tragic Years," "Goodbye, Broad-
way—Hello, Hello," "Problem No. 4," "The Peril in the Streets," "The
Sorcerer's Balm," "The Man Who Was Very Homesick for New York."

The World of Apples. New York: Alfred A. Knopf, 1973; reprint, New York:
Warner, 1974. "The Fourth Alarm," "The Jewels of the Cabots,"
"Percy," "Artemis, the Honest Well Digger," "The Chimera," "Mene,
Mene, Tekel, Upharsin," "Montraldo," "Three Stories," "The Geometry
of Love," "The World of Apples."

Novels

Bullet Park. New York: Alfred A. Knopf, 1969. Reprint, New York: Bantam,
1970; Ballantine, 1978.

Selected Bibliography

Falconer. New York: Alfred A. Knopf: 1977; Boston: G. K. Hall (Adult Series Large Print Books), 1977; reprint, New York: Ballantine, 1978.
Oh What a Paradise It Seems. New York: Alfred A. Knopf, 1982.
The Wapshot Chronicle. New York: Harper & Brothers, 1957. Reprint, New York: Penguin, 1963; Bantam, 1964; Time-Life, 1965; Harper & Row, 1973. Reprint with *The Wapshot Scandal* in single volume, New York: Harper & Row, 1979.
The Wapshot Scandal. New York: Harper & Row, 1964. Reprint, New York: Bantam, 1965; Harper & Row, 1973.

Short Fiction in Periodicals and Other Anthologies

"Bullet Park." *New Yorker* 43 (25 November 1967):56–59. Chapter 1 of *Bullet Park*.
"Christmas Eve at St. Botolph's." *New Yorker* 37 (23 December 1961):26–31. Chapter 1 of *The Wapshot Scandal*.
"The Clear Haven." *New Yorker* 32 (1 December 1956):50–111. Chapters 29 and 31 of *The Wapshot Chronicle.*
"The Embarkment for Cythera." *New Yorker* 38 (3 November 1962):59–106. Chapter 5 of *The Wapshot Scandal*. Also in *Prize Stories 1964: The O. Henry Awards*, edited by Richard Poirier (Garden City, N.Y.: Doubleday, 1964), and *First-Prize Stories of 1919–1966*, edited by Harry Hansen (Garden City, N.Y.: Hanover House, 1966).
"Falconer." *Ladies Home Journal* 94 (July 1977):115–16. From chapter 3.
"Falconer." *Playboy* 23 (January 1976):150–54, 188–92. Chapter 1.
"The Folding-Chair Set." *New Yorker* 51 (13 October 1975):36–38. Portions from *Falconer*.
"Independence Day at St. Botolph's." *New Yorker* 30 (3 July 1954):18–23. Chapter 1 of *The Wapshot Chronicle*. Also in *Problems in Prose*, edited by Paul Haines (New York: Harper & Row, 1963).
"The International Wilderness." *New Yorker* 39 (6 April 1963):43–47. Chapter 19 of *The Wapshot Scandal*.
"The Journal of an Old Gent." *New Yorker* 31 (18 February 1956):32–59. Chapters 14 and 16 of *The Wapshot Chronicle*. Also in *Prize Stories 1957: The O. Henry Awards*, edited by Paul Engle and Constance Urdang (Garden City, N.Y.: Doubleday, 1957).
"The Leaves, the Lion-Fish and the Bear." *Esquire* 82 (November 1974):110–11, 192–96. Portion from *Falconer*.
"Miss Wapshot." *New Yorker* 32 (22 September 1956):40–43. Chapter 6 of *The Wapshot Chronicle*.
"Playing Fields." *Playboy* 15 (July 1968):76–78, 84, 164–65. Chapter 6 of *Bullet Park*. Also in *The Pocket Playboy: Number Two* (Chicago: Playboy, 1973).
"The Traveller." *New Yorker* 37 (9 December 1961):50–58. Chapter 17 of *The Wapshot Scandal*.

Selected Bibliography

"The Wapshot Scandal." *Esquire* 60 (July 1963):52–54. Chapter 29 of *The Wapshot Scandal.*
"The Yellow Room." *Playboy* 15 (January 1968):87–92, 217–224. Chapter 14 of *Bullet Park.* Also in *The Best from Playboy: Number Five* (Chicago: Playboy, 1971); *Masks* (Chicago: Playboy, 1971); and *The Twentieth Anniversary Playboy Reader*, edited by Hugh M. Hefner (Chicago: Playboy, 1974).

Other Writings

"Author's Note." in *Stories*, a joint collection with Jean Stafford, Daniel Fuchs, and William Maxwell. New York: Farrar, Straus & Cudahy, 1956; New York: Farrar, Straus & Giroux, 1966.
"Cheever's Letters." A series of letters (1933–56) to Elizabeth Ames, director of Yaddo. In *Vanity Fair* 47 (May 1984):62–65.
"Fiction Is Our Most Intimate Means of Communication." *U.S. News and World Report* 86 (21 May 1979):92.
"F. Scott Fitzgerald." In *Atlantic Brief Lives*, edited by Louis Kronenberger, 275–276. Boston: Little, Brown, 1971.
"In Praise of Readers." *Parade*, 28 December 1980, 6.
The Letters of John Cheever, edited by Benjamin Cheever. New York: Simon & Schuster, 1988.
Preface to *The Short Stories of John Cheever*. New York: Alfred A. Knopf, 1978. vii–viii.
The Shady Hill Kidnapping. A play presented by PBS as part of the *American Playhouse* series, 12 January 1982.
"What Happened." In *Understanding Fiction*, 2d ed., edited by Cleanth Brooks and Robert Penn Warren, 570–72. New York: Appleton-Century-Crofts, 1959.
"Why I Write Short Stories." *Newsweek* 92 (30 October 1978):24–25.
"A Word from Writer Directly to Reader." In *Fiction of the Fifties*, edited by Herbert Gold, 21. Garden City, N.Y.: Doubleday & Co., 1959.

Secondary Works

Interviews

Beisch, June. "John Cheever Comes Home." *Boston Herald Magazine* 28 August 1977.
Benidt, Bruce. "Conversations with John Cheever." *Minneapolis Star*, 30 December 1978, 9–12.
Brans, Jo. "Stories to Comprehend Life." *Southwest Review* 65 (Autumn 1980):337–45.
Breit, Harvey. "Big Interruption." *New York Times Book Review*, 10 May 1953, 8.

Selected Bibliography

Cowley, Susan Cheever. "A Duet of Cheevers." *Newsweek* 89 (14 March 1977):61–71.

Donaldson, Scott. *Conversations with John Cheever.* Jackson: University Press of Mississippi, 1987.

Fullerton, Mabelle. "Quincy Youth Is Achieving New York Literary Career." *Quincy Patriot-Ledger,* 6 August 1940, 1, 7.

Gilder, Joshua. "John Cheever's Affirmation of Faith." *Saturday Review* 9 (March 1982):16–19.

Gioia, Dana, Millicent Dillon, and Michael Stillman. "An Interview with John Cheever." *Sequoia* (a Stanford University publication) 20 (Summer–Autumn 1976):29–35.

Grant, Annette. "John Cheever: The Art of Fiction LXII." *Paris Review* 17 (Fall 1976):39–66.

Gutwillig, Robert. "Dim Views through Fog." *New York Times Book Review,* 13 November 1960, 68–69.

Hersey, John. "John Hersey Talks with John Cheever." *Yale Alumni Magazine and Journal,* December 1977, 21–24. Reprinted in part as "John Cheever, Boy and Man," *New York Times Book Review,* 26 March 1978, 3, 31–34.

———. "Talk with John Cheever." *New York Times Book Review,* 6 March 1977, 1, 24, 26–28.

Janeway, Elizabeth. "Is the Short Story Necessary?" In *The Writer's World,* edited by Elizabeth Janeway. New York: McGraw-Hill, 1969. Reprinted in *Short Story Theories,* edited by Charles E. May, 94–106. Athens: Ohio University Press, 1976.

Munro, Eleanor. "Not Only I, the Narrator, but I John Cheever." *Ms.* 5 (April 1977):74–77, 105.

Nichols, Lewis. "A Visit with John Cheever." *New York Times Book Review,* 5 January 1964, 28.

Robb, Christina. "Cheever's Story." *Boston Globe Magazine,* 6 July 1980, 11–13, 27–31, 35.

Seligson, Marcia. "Portrait of a Man Reading." *Washington Post Book World,* 9 March 1969, 2.

Valhouli, James. "Interview with John Cheever," a transcription of a discussion held at Bradford College, 2 December 1977.

Note: Several of the interviews listed here are reprinted in Donaldson's collection.

Bibliographies

Bosha, Francis J. *John Cheever: A Reference Guide.* Boston: G. K. Hall, 1981.

Coates, Dennis. "A Cheever Bibliographical Supplement, 1978–81." In *Critical Essays on John Cheever,* edited by R. G. Collins, 279–85. Boston: G. K. Hall, 1982. Together with the checklist (next item), an indispensable guide for students; comprehensive through 1981.

————. "John Cheever: A Checklist, 1930–1978." *Bulletin of Bibliography* 36 (January–March 1979):1–13, 49.

Morace, Robert. "John Cheever." *Contemporary Authors: Bibliographical Series* 1 (1986):157–92. Indispensable guide for students; includes a valuable critical study of scholarship through 1984.

Trakas, Deno. "John Cheever: An Annotated Secondary Bibliography (1943–1978)." *Resources for American Literary Study* 9 (1979):181–199.

Biographies

Cheever, Susan. *Home Before Dark*. Boston: Houghton Mifflin, 1984.

Donaldson, Scott. *John Cheever*. New York: Random House, 1988.

Critical Studies

Coale, Samuel. *John Cheever*. New York: Ungar, 1977.

Collins, R. G., ed. *Critical Essays on John Cheever*. Boston: G. K. Hall, 1982.

Hunt, George. *John Cheever: The Hobgoblin Company of Love*. Grand Rapids: William B. Eerdmans, 1983.

Waldeland, Lynne. *John Cheever*. Boston: Twayne, 1979.

Articles, Reviews, and Parts of Books

Aldridge, John W. "John Cheever and the Soft Sell of Disaster." In *Time to Murder and Create*, 171–77. New York: David McKay Co., 1966.

Allen, Walter. *The Short Story in English*, 367–71. New York: Oxford University Press, 1981.

Auser, Cortland P. "John Cheever's Myth of Man and Time: 'The Swimmer.'" *CEA Critic* 29 (March 1967):18–19.

Bidney, Martin. "'The Common Day' and the Immortality Ode: Cheever's Wordsworthian Craft." *Studies in Short Fiction* 23 (Spring 1986):139–51.

Blythe, Hal, and Charlie Sweet. "Classical Allusions in John Cheever's 'The Swimmer.'" *Notes on Modern American Literature* 8 (Spring–Summer 1984):item 1.

Bracher, Frederick. "John Cheever and Comedy." *Critique* 6 (Spring 1963):66–77.

Burt, Struthers. "John Cheever's Sense of Drama." *Saturday Review* 26 (24 April 1943):9. Included in Collins.

Chesnick, Eugene. "The Domesticated Stroke of John Cheever." *New England Quarterly* 44 (December 1971):531–52. Included in Collins.

Coles, Robert. "Gatsby at the B School." *New York Times Book Review*, 25 October 1987, 1, 40–41.

Collins, R. G. "From Subject to Object and Back Again: Individual Identity in John Cheever's Fiction." *Twentieth Century Literature* 28 (Summer 1982):1–13.

Selected Bibliography

Cowley, Malcolm. "John Cheever: The Novelist's Life as a Drama." *Sewanee Review* 91 (Winter 1983):1–16.

DeMott, Benjamin. "A Grand Gatherum of Some Late Twentieth Century Weirdos." *New York Times Book Review*, 27 April 1969, 1, 40–41.

Donaldson, Scott. "John Cheever." In *American Writers: A Collection of Literary Biographies*, edited by Leonard Ungar, Supp. 1, Part 1, 174–99. New York: Scribner's, 1979.

————. "The Machines in Cheever's Garden." In *The Changing Face of the American Suburbs*, edited by Barry Schwartz, 309–22, 336–37. Chicago: University of Chicago Press, 1976. Included in Collins.

Edwards, Paul C. "Transforming Cheever: Three Failures in Reimagination." *Literature in Performance* 5 (April 1985):14–26.

Facknitz, Mark A. R. "Missing the Train: Raymond Carver's Sequel to John Cheever's 'The Five-Forty-Eight.'" *Studies in Short Fiction* 22 (Summer 1985):345–47.

Gardner, John. "A Cheever Milestone: 61 Elegantly Crafted Stories." *Chicago Tribune Book World*, 22 October 1978, 1.

Gerlach, John. "Closure in Modern Short Fiction: Cheever's 'The Enormous Radio' and 'Artemis, the Honest Well Digger,'" *Modern Fiction Studies* 28 (Spring 1982):145–52.

Gilder, Joshua. "John Cheever's Affirmation of Faith." *Saturday Review* 9 (March 1982):16–19.

Hardwick, Elizabeth. "Cheever, or The Ambiguities." *New York Review of Books* 32 (20 December 1984):3–4, 6, 8.

Hunt, George. "Beyond the Cheeveresque: A Style Both Lyrical and Idiosyncratic." *Commonweal* 106 (19 January 1979):20–22.

Irving, John. "Facts of Living." *Saturday Review* 5 (30 September 1978):44–46.

Kapp, Isa. "The Cheerless World of John Cheever." *New Leader* 61 (11 September 1978):16–17.

Kazin, Alfred. "O'Hara, Cheever and Updike." *New York Review of Books* 20 (19 April 1973):14–18. Reprinted in his *Bright Book of Life: American Novelists and Storytellers from Hemingway to Mailer*, 110–14. Boston: Little, Brown, 1973. Included in Collins.

Lee, Alwyn. "Ovid in Ossining." *Time* 83 (27 March 1964):66–72.

Leonard, John. "Cheever Country." *New York Times Book Review*, 7 March 1982, 1, 25–26.

————. "Cheever to Roth to Malamud." *Atlantic Monthly* 231 (June 1973):112–16.

Liberman, M. M. "Stasis, Story, and Anti-Story." *Georgia Review* 39 (Fall 1985):527–33.

Mason, Michael. "Gilt-Edged Investments." *Times Literary Supplement*, 7 December 1979, 103.

Selected Bibliography

O'Hara, James. "John Cheever's Flowering Forth: The Breakthroughs of 1947." *Modern Language Studies* 17 (Fall 1987):50–59.

Peden, William. *The American Short Story: Continuity and Change 1940–1975.* Boston: Houghton Mifflin, 1975.

Reilly, Edward. "Saving Grace and Moral Balance in John Cheever's Stories." *Publications of the Mississippi Philological Association* 1 (Summer 1982):24–29.

Stengel, Wayne. "John Cheever's Surreal Vision and the Bridge of Language." *Twentieth Century Literature* 33 (Summer 1987):223–33.

Ten Harmsel, Henrietta. "'Young Goodman Brown' and 'The Enormous Radio.'" *Studies in Short Fiction* 9 (Fall 1972):407–8.

Towers, Robert. "Light Touch." *New York Review of Books* 25 (9 November 1978):3–4.

Tyler, Anne. "Books Considered." *New Republic* 179 (4 November 1978):45–47.

Waldeland, Lynne. "Isolation and Integration: John Cheever's 'The Country Husband.'" *Ball State University Forum* 27 (Winter 1986):5–11.

Walkiewicz, E. P. "1957–1968: Toward Diversity of Form." In *The American Short Story, 1945–1980: A Critical History,* ed. Gordon Weaver, 35–40. Boston: Twayne, 1983.

Weaver, John D. "John Cheever: Recollections of a Childlike Imagination." *Los Angeles Times Book Review,* 13 March 1977, 3, 8.

Index

Index

Daedalus, 61
Dante, 8
DeMott, Benjamin, 72
De Vries, Peter, 135
Dickens, Charles, 109, 112, 134
Didion, Joan, 130–31
Donne, John, 110
Donaldson, Scott, 71–72, 128–32
Dos Passos, John, 117
Dugan, Alan, 110

Eliot, George, 112
Eliot, T. S., 20, 46, 110

Fall, The, 111
Fathers and Sons, 7
Faulkner, William, 75, 84, 110, 131
Fitzgerald, F. Scott, 3, 5, 75, 130–31
Flaubert, Gustave, 65–66, 111, 113
France, Anatole, 125
"From Parallels to Paradise . . . ,"
    137–45
Frost, Robert, 110
Fullerton, Mabelle, 104

Galsworthy, John, 124
Gardner, John, 130
Garrett, George, 130
Gibbon, Edward, 112
Gogol, Nikolai, 111, 134
Goldwyn, Sam, 50
Grant, Annette, 68

Harper's Bazaar, 104
Hawthorne, Nathaniel, 30, 42, 47,
    61, 139
"Heart Is a Lonely Hunter, The,"
    105
Heller, Joseph, 130
Hemingway, Ernest, 5, 75, 84, 110
Henderson the Rain King, 112
Hersey, John, 31, 114–20, 130, 143
Holroyd, Michael, 109
Homer, 61
Hopper, Edward, 59
Hunt, George, 132–37

Irving, John, 46

Jakobson, Roman, 138
James, William, 119
"John Cheever, Boy and Man," 114–
    20
"John Cheever," 128–32
"John Cheever's Sense of Drama,"
    124–26
Johnson, Samuel, 61
Jones, James, 18
Joyce, James, 17, 109

Kafka, Franz, 85, 131
Kazin, Alfred, 58, 79, 126–30
Keats, John, 36
Kierkegaard, Soren, 134–35
Kipling, Rudyard, 125

Lardner, Ring, 135
Left, The, 5
Leonard, John, 10
Life With Father, 19

Madame Bovary, 111, 113
Mailer, Norman, 112
Marquand, J. P., 130
Mather, Cotton, 30
Maupassant, Guy de, 125
Maxwell, William, 25
"Maypole of Marymount, The," 30
McCullers, Carson, 105
Merchant of Venice, The, 109
Michelangelo, 36
Moorehead, Alan, 112
Morace, Robert, 137–45
My Antonia, 112
"My Last Duchess," 28

Nabokov, Vladimir, 130
New Masses, 117
New Republic, 3, 5, 96, 97, 114
New Yorker, 5–6, 13, 16, 17, 21, 23,
    25, 37–41, 57, 71, 97, 104, 125,
    126–32, 144
New York Times, 72, 79
Newsweek, 80

160

The Author

James E. O'Hara is an assistant professor of English at the Pennsylvania State University's York campus, where he teaches composition, creative writing, and introductory literature courses. He was a teaching fellow at the University of Michigan, where he received his Ph.D. in 1974. He served in Vietnam as an intelligence officer attached to U.S. Special Forces and has worked as a news reporter and detective. In addition to several articles on John Cheever, he has published studies of John O'Hara, William Shakespeare, and Sir Philip Sidney. He lives in York, Pennsylvania, with his wife, Ellen, daughter Stephanie, son Matthew, and cat Dandelion.

The Editor

General editor Gordon Weaver earned his B.A. in English at the University of Wisconsin-Milwaukee in 1961; his M.A. in English at the University of Illinois, where he studied as a Woodrow Wilson Fellow, in 1962; and his Ph.D. in English and creative writing at the University of Denver in 1970. He is the author of several novels, including *Count a Lonely Cadence*, *Give Him a Stone*, *Circling Byzantium*, and *The Eight Corners of the World*. Many of his numerous short stories are collected in *The Entombed Man of Thule*, *Such Waltzing Was Not Easy*, *Getting Serious*, *Morality Play*, and *A World Quite Round*. Recognition of his fiction includes the St. Lawrence Award for Fiction (1973), two National Endowment for the Arts fellowships (1974 and 1989), and the O. Henry First Prize (1979). He edited *The American Short Story, 1945–1980: A Critical History*. He is a professor of English at Oklahoma State University and serves as an adjunct member of the faculty of the Vermont College Master of Fine Arts in Writing Program. Married, and the father of three daughters, he lives in Stillwater, Oklahoma.